British Histor
General Edito

PUBLISH.

Further titles are in preparation

MEDIEVAL SCOTLAND

THE MAKING OF AN IDENTITY

BRUCE WEBSTER

First published in Great Britain 1997 by
MACMILLAN PRESS LTD
Houndmills, Basingstoke, Hampshire RG21 6XS
and London
Companies and representatives throughout the world

A catalogue record for this book is available from the British Library.

ISBN 0–333–56760–9 hardback
ISBN 0–333–56761–7 paperback

First published in the United States of America 1997 by
ST. MARTIN'S PRESS, INC.,
Scholarly and Reference Division,
175 Fifth Avenue, New York, N.Y. 10010

ISBN 0–312–16519–6

Library of Congress Cataloging-in-Publication Data
Webster, Bruce.
Medieval Scotland : the making of an identity / Bruce Webster.
    p.   cm.
Includes bibliographical references and index.
ISBN 0–312–16519–6 (cloth)
1. Scotland—History—1057–1603.   2. Scotland—History—War of
Independence, 1285–1371.   3. National characteristics, Scottish.
4. Nationalism—Scotland—History.   5. Civilization, Medieval.
I. Title.
DA779.W43   1997
941.1—dc20   96–30739
                                                   CIP

This book is printed on paper suitable for recycling and made from fully managed and sustained forest sources.

10   9   8   7   6   5   4   3   2   1
06   05   04   03   02   01   00   99   98   97

Printed in Hong Kong

For Maddy

CONTENTS

ACKNOWLEDGEMENTS

An essay on such a wide subject as this involves many obligations. I hope my debts to the publications of others are acknowledged in the references which follow the text. I would like, however, particularly to thank the Historical Association for its very ready permission to make use of passages from the translation of the Declaration of Arbroath by Professor A. A. M. Duncan, which originally appeared in the Historical Association pamphlet *The Nation of Scots and the Declaration of Arbroath.*

Beyond these specific debts, I have received help from very many friends who have shared their thoughts on the problems of Scottish history. The annual meetings of the Scottish Medievalists at Pitlochry over the years have given me many ideas which I have worked on, almost unconsciously, without being able to make individual attributions or acknowledgements. Norman Macdougall and Roger Mason, at the University of St Andrews where I acted for four years as external examiner, and the students whose exam papers and dissertations I read, have given me many ideas, and corrected many others which I previously held. As one who has never taught Scottish history, I found the experience of examining it not only very pleasant but one from which I learned a great deal.

In addition, Roger Mason has read the entire typescript and has made very helpful suggestions for its improvement, of which I hope I have taken full advantage. I must also thank my colleague Alf Smyth at the University of Kent, for the many talks he has given over the years on early Scottish history, and for the chance to discuss its problems. The period is basic to my theme, but not one that I know at first hand, and I am very grateful for his guidance. Neither he nor Roger Mason, however, has any responsibility for what I have eventually written!

Finally, without the help of my wife this book would never have been completed. She has read draft after draft, clarifying what I was trying to say, pointing out where I was assuming knowledge of facts that should have been in the text, and helping to tidy up the style. My readers will hardly realise how much they owe to her. The dedication has been very thoroughly earned.

MAPS

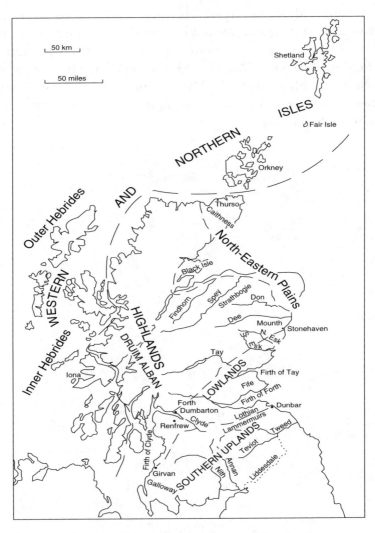

Map 1   The historic regions of Scotland

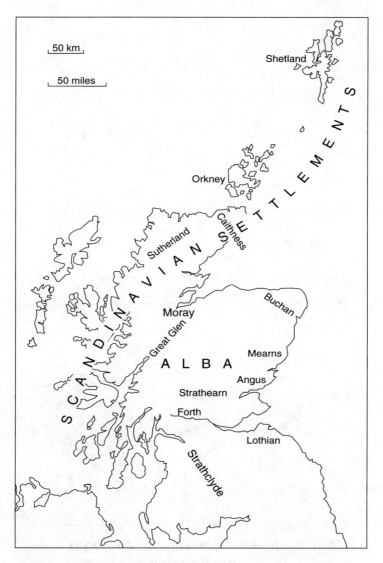

Map 2   The kingdom of Alba in the eleventh century

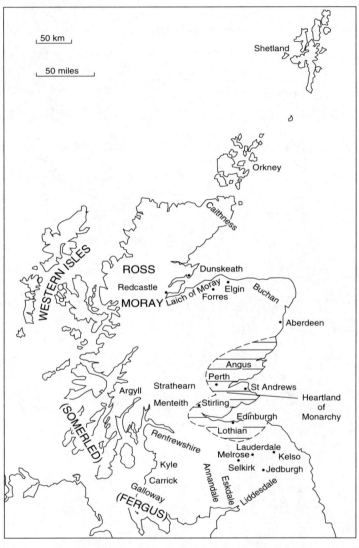

Map 3   The development of royal authority in the twelfth century

Map 4   The wars of independence, 1296–1357

GENEALOGICAL TABLES

The Descendants of Duncan I
Kings of Scots

(Kings of Scots and Queen Margaret 'Maid of Norway' are shown in capitals with the dates of their reigns)

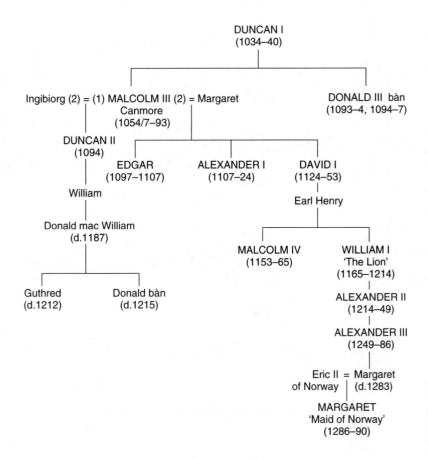

DUNCAN I
(1034–40)

Ingibiorg (2) = (1) MALCOLM III (2) = Margaret
Canmore
(1054/7–93)

DONALD III bàn
(1093–4, 1094–7)

DUNCAN II
(1094)

EDGAR
(1097–1107)

ALEXANDER I
(1107–24)

DAVID I
(1124–53)

William

Earl Henry

Donald mac William
(d.1187)

MALCOLM IV
(1153–65)

WILLIAM I
'The Lion'
(1165–1214)

Guthred
(d.1212)

Donald bàn
(d.1215)

ALEXANDER II
(1214–49)

ALEXANDER III
(1249–86)

Eric II = Margaret
of Norway | (d.1283)

MARGARET
'Maid of Norway'
(1286–90)

The Succession to the Crown in 1290

(Kings of Scots and Queen Margaret 'Maid of Norway' are shown in capitals with the dates of their reigns)

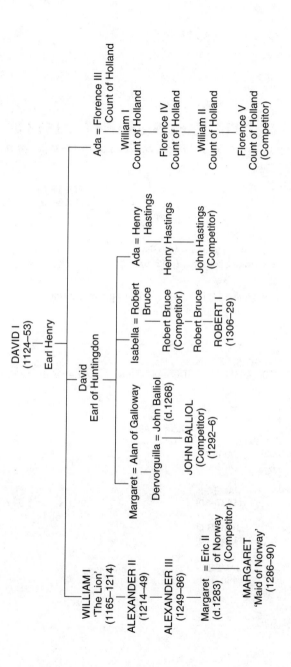

The Early Stewarts (to 1513)

(Kings of Scots are shown in capitals with the dates of their reigns)

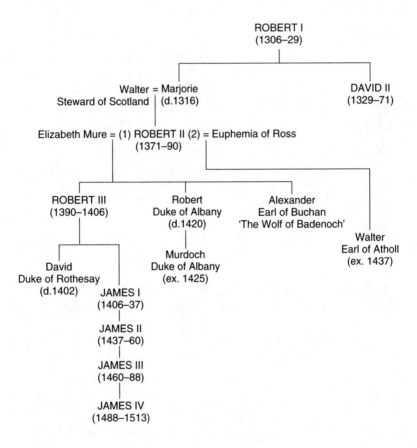

ROBERT I
(1306–29)

Walter = Marjorie
Steward of Scotland | (d.1316)

DAVID II
(1329–71)

Elizabeth Mure = (1) ROBERT II (2) = Euphemia of Ross
(1371–90)

ROBERT III
(1390–1406)

Robert
Duke of Albany
(d.1420)

Alexander
Earl of Buchan
'The Wolf of Badenoch'

Walter
Earl of Atholl
(ex. 1437)

David
Duke of Rothesay
(d.1402)

Murdoch
Duke of Albany
(ex. 1425)

JAMES I
(1406–37)

JAMES II
(1437–60)

JAMES III
(1460–88)

JAMES IV
(1488–1513)

INTRODUCTION:
THE PROBLEM OF A
SCOTTISH IDENTITY

Scotland ceased to be a distinct political entity with the Act of Union in 1707. Much of its structure was preserved, a distinct legal system and a distinct national church. But the essential element in the nineteenth-century concept of nationalism, an effective power of self-government, has not been available to Scots since the early eighteenth century.

Yet the sense of a Scottish identity is clearly alive, even though modern Scots have shown no overwhelming enthusiasm for formal self-government. The Scottish National Party and similar movements in the present century have often served as a focus for protest votes against the remoteness of British government, a protest just as likely to be expressed by voting for British opposition parties. That has been the pattern in most elections since the late nineteenth century, and remained so even in the election of 1992, which during the campaign produced signs of a quite strong consciously Scottish feeling.

But Scotland remains distinct, not only in geography, but in architecture, society and culture, as can be experienced as soon as one crosses the Border. Scottish towns have a different feel and aspect from English. It is worth asking how this comes about and what are the elements which make up this distinctness, which is more a matter of a sense of a separate identity than of 'national' feeling in the nineteenth-century sense. For Scotland is not alone. The modern world in Europe and beyond has many identities which are not reflected in the political structures of post-Versailles Europe or of post-colonial Africa and Asia. They can at times be potent and destructive forces, as we see in former Yugoslavia and in many former colonies in Africa. In the British Isles, the Welsh, who have not been an independent nation since 1283, have at least as strong a sense of identity as the Scots; as have the Bretons in France, and the Catalans and Basques in Spain. The question of identities is of some importance in the modern world. We need a clearer understanding of their nature and their sources; and though no nation can be taken as typical, the Scots are an interesting example which may help to understand a much wider phenomenon.

As we shall see in a later chapter, the Scottish identity is rooted neither in geography nor race. As a land, Scotland is thoroughly diverse, divided rather than united by geography. It was a land of many peoples, Scots, Picts, British, English and Norse in the Dark Ages, with later additions of Norman-French and Flemings. Nor is there a single 'native' Scottish language: there are at least two – Gaelic and Scots. Southern English has now largely replaced Scots. This is partly a result of the dominance of the English Bible (the first widely read translation of any part of the Bible into Scots was only published in 1983!)[1] and still more the result of social and economic developments of the nineteenth and twentieth centuries. Gaelic has now retreated to the Western Isles and parts of the Highland mainland. Throughout its independent history, however, Scotland has always been a multicultural society; and there is no point in trying to establish any of its components as more truly 'Scots' than the others.

Whence then and when came this sense of identity? The inhabitants of what was to be Scotland had no such sense, so far as we can tell, when they faced the Romans under Agricola in the first century AD. We have to depend on erratically spread notices by Roman writers who knew little if anything of the realities of life outside the frontiers, but all the evidence suggests fluctuating tribal societies, some of which, such as the Brigantes, straddled what was later to be the Borders. Tacitus, indeed, in his account of the battle of *Mons Graupius*, writes as if Calgacus, whom he represents as leader of the Caledonians, was at the head of a tribal coalition; but the evidence of later Irish, Scottish and Pictish royal genealogies and chronicles makes it clear that any permanent unity was far in the future.

Two things very gradually worked to bring disparate peoples together: first the increasing acceptance of a single faith, as Christian missionaries in the sixth to ninth centuries gradually converted the different tribes; and the even more gradual ascendancy from the ninth century of a single line of kings, who ruled over Picts and Scots as the kingdom of Alba. The Scandinavian invasions, from the ninth century onwards, affected Scotland in two ways. The Scandinavian settlements in the north and west had the effect of forcing together the Picts, long settled in the north-east, and the Scots, who had come from Ireland in the sixth century to settle the west and central areas, into a defensive union. At the same time, the Scandinavian settlements in eastern Ireland and northern England, the kingdoms of Dublin and York, temporarily isolated the Scoto-Pictish realm what might otherwise have been an expanding and threatening kingdom of Wessex and England. This gave the Picts and Scots the opportunity and necessity of consolidating their union and gradually, by the eleventh century, expanding it to include the Anglians of Lothian and the Britons of Strathclyde. Hence by the time the kings of Wessex were able in the tenth century to extend their power into the north of England, there was already a reasonably consolidated and expanding authority in Scotland.

As late as the eleventh century, however, the kings of Scots were still little more than 'high-kings' ruling a collection of peoples in regions which all saw themselves as distinct and whose local rulers often saw themselves at least as under-kings (in Galloway and the Western Isles as late as the twelfth century). Macbeth, a ruler of Moray in the eleventh century, even succeeded for seventeen years in displacing the established line. Hardly any later 'rebellions' were successful, but they still happened down to the early thirteenth century.

How did this tribal society, divided as it was by geography, race and language, come to acquire a sense of a single identity?

In the first place, Scotland, like France, retained a single dynasty which ruled from the final establishment of Malcolm Canmore in 1057 until the death of Alexander III in 1286, apart from a few years after Malcolm's death in 1093. The Canmore dynasty did not survive as long as the Capetians who ruled France from 987 to 1328, but the effect was the same. Their power spanned exactly the period when European monarchies were developing systems of government and administration to bind their realms together in a way which earlier medieval monarchies had been unable to do. Each dynasty worked in its own fashion: Scottish government was different in structure from that of the Anglo-Norman kings or of the Capetians, but like theirs it succeeded in welding a loose authority into a lasting entity (See chapter 2).

Secondly, the Scottish church had a special part to play. As in England, a single faith long anticipated a single polity and, like the secular power, the church too was cut off in the ninth century from southern influence by the intrusion of pagan Scandinavians. We know little that is precise about the Scottish church of the tenth and eleventh centuries, but when it emerged from obscurity in the twelfth century, the church of Strathclyde which extended from the Firth of Clyde to Cumbria was not yet fully integrated with that of the rest of Scotland. Nevertheless, the Scottish church was determined to uphold its independence as a separate province from those of York and Canterbury. Churchmen were literate and articulate: and this stand against outside interference is the first explicit expression which has come down to us of a sense of a Scottish indentity which covered the bulk of what we now recognise as Scotland (see Chapter 3).

By 1286, when Alexander III, the last adult king in the line of Malcolm Canmore, died, the Scottish identity was supported by a national monarchy and a national church. The disputed succession which followed Alexander's death, and the subsequent conflict with England, challenged that sense of identity and threatened it with a rival British identity which, in the hands of Edward I, amounted to little more than English imperialism. The result was a series of wars which opened divisions within Scotland – the 'Wars of Independence' have sometimes been seen as a civil 'War of the Scots'. The struggle lasted at least until 1357 but its effect was ultimately to reinforce the sense of Scottish national identity and link it with a hostility towards England which long outlasted these wars. This hostility seriously complicated the politics of the sixteenth and seventeenth centuries, and threatened the success of the union of 1707. That union long remained profoundly unpopular in Scotland. Riots in Glasgow in 1725 against the new Malt Tax and the Porteous riots in Edinburgh in 1736 both reflected a hostility to what was seen as 'English' domination. That hostility was increased by the ill-considered efforts of the government at repression.

Growing economic prosperity and the new opportunities in the developing 'British' empire, which sprang from the Seven Years' War against France, seemed likely in the late eighteenth century to introduce a new sense of a 'British' identity which might in time have replaced the Scottish. This was at a time when Edinburgh was one of the leading intellectual centres of the Enlightenment; when a Scot, Allan Ramsay, was one of the best British portrait painters; when Robert Adam was not only building mansions in Scotland but throughout England as well; and when David Hume, who remained in Scotland, was trying to purge his speech of all provincial Scotticisms. Paradoxically, the 'enlightened' Scots seemed in some danger of emasculating the idea of a Scottish identity.

But national identities depend very heavily on perceptions and even myths about the past. As we shall see in chapters 4 and 5, the response of Scots in the middle ages to the English threat was to develop a mythological past and a line of kings going back to the founders of Scotland in prehistoric times, a past which emphasised and served to establish Scotland's ancient integrity and independence. Since this mythology had no sound historical basis, it was destroyed by the scientific historical techniques of the seventeenth and eighteenth centuries. But the romantic movement re-awakened a sense of the past. Sir Walter Scott was brought up in the 1770s with the Border Ballads, stories of past adventures in some of which his own ancestors were involved. He responded to tales of chivalry and began his career as a writer by collecting and publishing what he could recover of the old ballads. He went on in his original poems and his finest novels to present Scotland's past in a way which made him one of the best-selling writers of the age. Thus he played his part in reviving the sense of a living Scottish identity. Scott was very aware of the danger to that identity and felt strongly the need to keep it alive. One such threat in 1826 was to the continuing existence of Scottish bank-notes. It is thanks at least in part to the campaign that Scott waged in the anonymous *Letters of Malachi Malagrowther* that Scotland kept its notes when all English banks save the Bank of England lost theirs. More seriously, Scott was one of the founders and chief encouragers of the Scottish historical clubs – a mixture of publishing societies and dining clubs. In the years from the late 1820s to the middle of the century these clubs produced many of the collections of documents and texts which we still use in the study of medieval Scottish history. Scott was the first president of the Bannatyne Club, the most prolific of all the clubs and, when he died in 1832, he was succeeded in office by his close friend Thomas Thomson, Deputy-Keeper of the Scottish Records. Scott's contribution to the revival of Scottish history and of a Scottish identity went far beyond his novels. He has often been accused of excessive romanticism; for, though his knowledge of Scottish history was deep and wide, his passion for the romantic could mislead him. It was Scott who planned the ceremonies surrounding the visit of George IV to Edinburgh in 1822 which became the occasion for a strange burst of tartanry: George IV himself appeared incongruously dressed as a highland chief! Scott bears some of the responsibility for many of the delusions which followed from this extravaganza, not least the sense that the Scottish identity was inextricably tied to the Highlands, the kilt and the bagpipes. Yet anyone who reads attentively *Waverley* or *Roy Roy* or the closing chapters of *The Heart of Midlothian* will see that Scott well knew that Scotland's identity had many strands of which the Highlanders were only one. Nevertheless, Scott's showmanship as well as his novels helped to restore the self-confidence of Scots in their continuing identity: his work also set Scottish history on the way to a revival which promised a sounder basis to this identity.

In the first half of the nineteenth century, Scotland was well in advance as a centre of historical studies. The clubs could not match the outstanding scholarship of the German *Monumenta* series, which is still the basis for any study of the early history of the medieval Empire; but the first of the Scottish clubs, the Bannatyne, was founded under Scott's presidency in 1823 only four years after the start of the *Monumenta* in 1819.

Sadly the effort did not last: by the middle of the century most of the clubs had given up or were failing, suffering from what has been called 'a failure of nerve'.[2] Perhaps this was because in the late nineteenth century the landed and professional classes who dominated the clubs were in retreat before the business men and entrepreneurs who were finding their profits in the Empire, and whose horizons were wider than Scotland. It may be that the passing of the Empire in the mid-twentieth century and the retreat from those overseas fields, had something to do with the striking revival of Scottish historical studies heralded by the work of W. Croft Dickinson at Edinburgh in the 1930s, and taking off after the Second World War in the work of a group of younger Scottish historians headed by Geoffrey Barrow and A. A. M. Duncan. Is it perhaps possible that both the lapse in the later nineteenth century and the revival in the second half of the twentieth are themselves a reflection of a fluctuating confidence, not in Scottish history but in Scottish identity? It may be significant that the first important sign of a revival in interest in the publication of Scottish historical texts came as early as 1886, with the foundation of the much more modern Scottish History Society, at a time when there were other signs of a reviving sense of Scottish identity. The first appointment of a Secretary of State for Scotland was made in 1885. It may also be significant that a Scottish identity is now sometimes seen as more closely linked to the ideal of Europe, an area with which Scotland has always had very close connections in education, in trade and in religion, both before and after the Reformation. Europe is a concept which has always been built on many distinct identities, and which depends on the individuality of its parts; while the concept of a British identity, ever since Edward I, has reflected a centralising tendency.

This book aims to trace the development of the sense of Scottish identity in the middle ages, and to analyse its sources. Beginning from the physical and ethnic diversity of the land of Scotland, it tries to follow the different elements which contributed to this identity and ends with a survey of Scotland's place in and contacts with a wider Europe on the eve of the Reformation, which was so greatly to change Scotland's external relations and the character of its sense of identity.

1

THE IDENTITY OF PLACE

Physically, Scotland is not a single entity: it is a land of many distinct and separate regions. If you look at a physical map of England, you can see that it belongs together. The lowlands to the south and east form a single area; and the higher regions, though they can be formidable, are, as it were, islands penetrated by lowland passages which lead a conqueror directly to all parts. From the Thames crossing which became London, there are direct routes to Yorkshire and up the east coast to Berwick; another opening leads to Liverpool and Chester, between the Pennines and the Welsh mountains, another to Cardiff and South Wales. Along these paths, Roman roads were built, Roman armies marched; and to this day, the roads and railways spread out from London, which was destined by geography to be the centre of a united country. Scotland is different. Geology splits the land into five areas: the Southern Uplands; a lowland belt between two faults, one running from Girvan in Ayrshire to Dunbar in East Lothian, the other from Dumbarton on the Clyde to Stonehaven, south of Aberdeen; the high and barren Highlands to north and west; the north-eastern coastal plains between the barrier of the Mounth, south of Aberdeen, and the limits of the plain of Caithness to the west of Thurso; and across the sea, the Hebrides, Orkney and Shetland. Even the lowland belt was divided in the middle ages by marshes in the

Forth valley, which split off the area round the Forth from the valley of the Clyde to the west; while the firths of Forth and Tay divide the eastern lowlands separating Lothian, Fife and Angus from one another.

Inhabited Scotland is mainly a land of coastal plains and river valleys. There is no single or obvious centre; and each region is separated from its neighbours either by seas, or by hills crossed only by high, sometimes difficult, often dangerous paths. The Tweed valley in the south-east, rising from the rich lands of the Merse around Berwick to the upland pastures of Tweedale and Teviotdale, is cut off in the east from Lothian by the Lammermuir Hills. Further north, Lothian is separated from Fife by the Firth of Forth, crossed by ferries at Queensferry and Earlsferry; Fife is divided from Angus by the Tay, bridged in the middle ages only at Perth; the heights of the Mounth, reaching the sea at Stonehaven, separate the north-eastern coastal plain from that to the south; and the same plain is cut off from the great region of Moray by the hills of Strathbogie; Caithness is separated from Moray by further hills, some reaching very close to the sea, to the alarm of incautious drivers to this day, who may be taken aback by a hairpin bend which proves to drop on one side straight to the sea far below! All these eastern coastal regions have in their hinterlands river valleys which reach far into the highland areas; valleys of Tweed and Teviot, Forth, Tay, North and South Esk, Dee and Don, Spey and Findhorn – all rise into progressively higher land, accessible for a distance from the coastal plains, but all ending in high, difficult and barren hills. The south-west again repeats the pattern in the lands around the Clyde, which divide into Dunbartonshire north of the river, Renfrewshire to the south and Lanarkshire in the interior further up the valley; and in Ayrshire and Galloway to the south – a series of river valleys, each a separate small region, all ending in high and barren lands. A drive or rail journey from Carlisle to Glasgow over Beattock summit is typical – the traveller sees Annandale narrow till he or she reaches the open moorland of the pass, which gradually sinks down again to more inhabited and planted land with the trees and fields of cultivation. Even in the 1990s, the sense of isolation is there, though now it attracts us. In earlier times it must have been a grim and dangerous land. To cross from Canonbie on the back road to Hawick up Liddesdale and to come on the stark bulk of Hermitage Castle in the open moorland gives a sense of a land barely controllable by the limited resources of the middle ages, a land where neither Scottish crown or English crown could rule with effect.

Many of the coastal areas tended to be linked outwards across the seas rather than to the rest of the mainland, for seas could be pathways as much as barriers. Galloway in the south west was on the shores of the Irish Sea, which in the early middle ages was a world to itself, encompassing southern Scotland, Ireland, Man, north-west England and parts of Wales extending round to the Bristol Channel. In early times Christianity crossed the Irish Sea on at least two occasions: in the fifth century, when St Patrick from Cumbria became the apostle of Ireland; and in the sixth when St Columba settled in Iona, to spread Irish Christian influence over the Western Isles and some of the mainland. Irish hermits arrived at the court of King Alfred of Wessex in the ninth century.[1] The politics of the tenth century are of full of movements across that sea. Kintyre is only some twenty miles from Ulster; and even in the later middle ages the affairs of Scotland and Ireland intermingled both in the Wars of Independence and in the early fifteenth century.

The western seaboard and the north-western and northern islands were part of series of far-flung Scandinavian settlements. From the eight century onwards, these reached round the islands and mainland of north-west Scotland; and in the ninth and tenth centuries across the North Atlantic to the Faeroes and Iceland, Greenland and even briefly to Labrador. Shetland, Orkney, Caithness and Sutherland, and parts of the Western Highlands and the Western Isles were drawn into a world very different from that of the Scottish glens and eastern coastal plains. The Western Isles might easily have

11

become part of a Norse sea-borne empire. Several kings of Norway may have had such an idea, but none was able to find the means to unite such wide-spread territories.

There was no ethnic cohesion in Scotland either. Even in prehistoric times, it was a melting pot of peoples. It was almost the end of the migratory road from the south. The *ultima Thule* of the ancient world seems to have been the Northern Isles, and Scotland was the last recipient of any invaders from the Mediterranean and western Europe. Beyond lay only the inhospitable seas, and only the Vikings and perhaps a few Celtic saints were to penetrate them. The earliest identifiable settlers in Scotland, apart from a few scattered meso-lithic communities, were the megalith builders of the third millennium BC, who seem to have come from the Mediterranean along the western seaboard via Spain, and left their monuments in the south-west, the Western Isles, Argyll and the north. Interestingly, later legend traced the Scots (for whom see below) as coming along just these routes.

The next main group were the Bronze-Age settlers who penetrated eastern Scotland from north-eastern England, perhaps sometime in the second millennium BC. In the last few centuries BC, the Celtic Iron-Age princes of the *La Tène* civilisation, the builders of Maiden Castle, Oldbury Hill and other sites in the south, established themselves in southern and eastern Scotland. They built notable forts at Traprain Law in East Lothian, and North Eildon in Roxburghshire and many elsewhere.[2] These last settlers may have dominated or composed the tribes recorded by Ptolemy in the second century AD, and were subjected to the Roman attempts at conquest which culminated in Agricola's victory at *Mons Graupius* (perhaps Bennachie in Aberdeenshire)[3] in AD 84. Agricola may have won the battle, but he was withdrawn by the Emperor Domitian too soon to win the campaign. The Romans found in Scotland a heterogeneous tribal society; and they left it much as it was. A scatter of coins and artifacts, and the mouldering remains of a good number of forts, which reached as far north as the coast of Moray, still mark the

Roman invasions. Their most important legacy to Scotland was a system of roads penetrating the southern uplands – Dere Street across at least to Newstead on the Tweed; roads up Annandale and Nithsdale, in the central lowlands, and further on at least to Perth. It is obvious that Edward I in his campaigns at the end of the thirteenth century, was following the Roman road up Nithsdale – the thirteenth-century castle of Tibbers on the estates of Drumlanrig has little point except to cover the Roman ford over the Nith where it is crossed by the road up Nithsdale – and these Roman roads are the ancestors of the A74, the A76 and the A9, as well as the modern railway lines. As elsewhere, the Roman engineers set the pattern for all later land communications.

Subsequently, the ethnic mix of Scotland was to become much more complex. When the British Isles were invaded in the fifth century by Germanic speaking tribes who settled in and dominated the south and eastern parts of the country, the Britons, the Iron-Age Celtic inhabitants who outlasted the Romans, were pushed into or left in the more mountainous western and north-western areas, Cornwall, Wales, Cumbria and what is now south-west Scotland. Germanic settlers, Angles, early established themselves in the fertile lands of the Vale of York and spread more slowly along the coastal regions of Northumbria. This left a British people in Cumbria and south-west Scotland, to form the British kingdom of Strathclyde which extended from Cumbria to the Clyde. For a time at the end of the sixth century it was threatened by an expanding Northumbria under the Anglian king Æthelfrith; and the influence of Northumbria is reflected in the Anglian-style carvings on the Ruthwell cross and Hoddam stones of the eighth century;[4] but the collapse of Northumbria at that period left Strathclyde secure for the moment. The Anglians, however, had, in the seventh century, already penetrated as far north as the Forth, and even briefly beyond it. That advance was halted by the defeat and death of King Egfrith in 685 at the battle of Nechtansmere (probably Dunnichen in Angus).

To the north of Forth and Clyde, there remained the society of the tribes listed by Ptolemy, headed by a Celtic aristocracy descended from those arrived from Gaul in the last millennium BC, the builders of the timber-laced forts which occur from Banffshire to Renfrewshire. These tribes are described as the *Caledonii* and from around AD 300 as the *Picti* (Picts) by Roman writers, terms which, it seems, refer collectively to a body of tribes which could, on occasions, as at the battle of *Mons Graupius*, act together. The 'problem of the Picts', of which so much has been written, appears to be a matter of terminology, and a terminology used by outsiders.[5] The name Picts occurs in Latin sources from AD 300 till the ninth century. At times, as with the Anglo-Saxons in southern Britain, there could be a single 'high-king' or overlord; at others, competing rulers. Whether there was ever a conscious 'Pictish' identity, recognised by all those we tend to describe as Picts, is doubtful; and from the late ninth century, the name Picts disappears. By then, we have sketchy native sources, in which the name of the kingdom is *Alba*, still the Gaelic term for Scotland. It is debatable whether anything more than the name 'Picts' disappeared, or whether the 'Picts' simply came to regard themselves as citizens of Alba. It is true that the distinctive 'symbol' stones (stones carved with strange recurrent symbols to whose meaning we have lost the clue) fade out after this time; but so did the typical styles of carving of Northumbria and, rather later, Ireland. So the disappearance of the symbols may not be particularly significant.

Into this essentially Celtic milieu, there came in the sixth century a rather different Celtic strain from Ireland, the 'Scots' from Antrim. Again there is a problem of names. Latin writers, referring to raids on late Roman Britain, mentioned, along with the 'Picts', the 'Scots', *Scoti*, by which name they describe those we would call Irish. The 'Scot' would have described himself as *Gàidheal* (Gael). 'Scots' is as much an outsider's description as 'Picts'. In the 5th century AD, the Scots were settled in Antrim; but they seem to have been a mobile people, ever on the look-out for new opportunities; and by AD 500, they were settling in the Inner Hebrides and western mainland of what was to be Scotland, from Ardnamurchan to Kintyre. There is some rather unconvincing evidence that these lands may have before been part of 'Pictland' (St Columba, who fled from Ireland to Iona in 565 is said by Bede to have been granted the island by the king of the Picts)[6] but by the late sixth century, the Scots were firmly established in the lands up to the central massif known as the 'Spine of Britain' or *Druim Alban*. Under their king Aedán, they were embarking on aggressive war against the Britons of Strathclyde, though they suffered a severe check in that quarter at the battle of Strath Carron (south-west of Stirling) in 642.[7] From then on, the 'Scots' and the 'Picts' seem to have been increasingly involved with one another, and indeed the Picts appeared to dominate, since several Picts are listed as kings of Scots in the king-lists.

The next addition to the ethnic mix came with the incursions and settlements of Scandinavians, moving south-west from Norway along the chain of islands via Shetland, Fair Isle and Orkney, on to the Western Isles of Scotland. Between the end of the eighth and the tenth centuries, the Scandinavians had established their settlements as far south as Cumbria and Dublin. The pressure from these new settlers seems to have pushed the Scots eastward: the islands and coastal areas were becoming less secure. The ultimate result, traditionally from 843 under Kenneth mac Alpin and his successors, was to create a united kingdom of Picts and Scots, two peoples who, under pressure, seem to have been merging for sometime. It is probably wrong to see that as a conquest, rather a natural reaction to external pressures. Indeed, contemporary Irish sources refer to Kenneth as 'king of the Picts'. In its own language, the kingdom was known as *Alba*, previously the Celtic term for Britain, as in 'Druim Alban'. Since 'England' was no longer British, Alba came to be restricted to what we now term as Scotland.[8] Alba, however, was not a term used in Latin sources, in which the Gaels (Irish or Scottish) were always the *Scoti*; and so, in the latinising world of the eleventh and twelfth centuries, *Scotia* became the name of the kingdom!

Scotland by the eleventh century was racially and linguistically mixed. There were English, British, Irish, Picts, Scandinavians, all speaking different languages: Anglo-Saxon, Brythonic, Gaelic, Pictish and Norse. Not until the twelfth century did 'Scots', a dialect of northern English, become the dominant language of most of the country south of the highland line. For far longer, Gaelic remained dominant in much of the highlands and in pockets elsewhere. Norse was common in the Western Isles at least till the thirteenth century, and dominant for much longer in Orkney and Shetland. If ethnic and linguistic identities had remained important, Scotland could easily have disappeared in the kinds of conflicts that have marked the collapse of former Yugoslavia. But it is far from clear that there was any general sense of Scottish identity even in embryonic form.

Scotland was also divided rather than united by the distribution of its natural resources. It was not that Scotland lacked resources: she was hardly richly endowed but there was, for so hilly a land, a considerable amount of good farming land, as is obvious to this day to anyone who journeys through East Lothian or Fife or the Mearns. Some at least of the higher ground was good pasture for sheep; other areas, to west and north, were good for cattle, and all round the coasts, and in many of the rivers, there was good fishing, as the frequent references to grants of fishing rights on rivers in monastic charters indicate. Newbattle Abbey, for instance, received from William the Lion, soon after the beginning of his reign in 1165, a confirmation of his predecessor's grant of Carmyle on the river Clyde 'with the waters and fishing rights belonging to the land'.[9] But all these resources were as scattered and disparate as the habitable land itself and so reinforced the natural divisions as disparate economies developed in different areas.

The Western Isles depended heavily, as they were to do for many centuries after the middle ages, on the harvest of the seas. But this locked the western highlands and islands into a sea-based economy, which turned their concerns to the west. The importance of ships to their lives emerges, to give two examples, both in the appearance of ship-service instead of knight-service in the land tenures of the area in the reign of Robert I;[10] and in the prominence of carvings of ships on the west-highland tombstones of the fifteenth and sixteenth centuries.[11] Small wonder that the economic as well as often the political contacts of the inhabitants were more with other lands around the western seas than with the rest of Scotland. Yet, even by medieval standards, it was not a very developed economy. It managed to support a limited number of lords, some of whom could build impressive stone castles, including some of the thirteenth century,[12] from which date there are few comparable examples elsewhere in the country; but no towns of consequence.

The economy of the far north is even more obscure. There is clear evidence, in both archaeology and place-names, for a dominant Scandinavian settlement in Shetland, Orkney, Caithness and Sutherland; and no question that, at least down to the thirteenth century, this whole region was closely linked into the Scandinavian political world. Contacts were close enough that in 1281 the daughter of Alexander III, King of Scots, married the Norwegian King Eric II. Norway itself was achieving by the twelfth century quite considerable economic development, despite a very unpromising terrain; a development based heavily on the sea, both as a resource to be exploited by fishing, and as a path to economic development by trade. Bergen in particular was already involved in extensive trade with north Germany, a trade which was quite often in the hands of Germans. The church in Norway had the resources to build impressive cathedrals in Stavanger and Trondheim, while the royal hall in thirteenth-century Bergen could scarcely be matched nearer than Westminster. Trade and the church had produced at least three important towns in twelfth-century Norway.

Did any of this apparent prosperity rub off on the Northern Isles and Caithness? At first sight there seems little evidence. Kirkwall Cathedral was certainly a striking building, if hardly the equal of Stavanger or Trondheim. But most Norse settlements in the north and west depended on subsistence farming; and, in this area, there is little sign of the trade that was bringing riches to Norway. It was the east coast not the north that seems to have exploited the trading potential of the north sea. We may be deceived by lack of evidence, but it appears that the Northern Isles were too far from any centres of wealth to develop a sophisticated trading economy and had to depend on their own soil and the sea for subsistence. In the history of both Scotland and Scandinavia they tend to be marginalised.

The situation changes on the east coast. The natural potential of the land itself increases: the Black Isle, not actually an island but the spur of land immediately to the north of Inverness, between the Moray Firth and the Cromarty Firth, has always been one of the most fertile parts of Scotland. The coastal plains and great river valleys of Moray and of Aberdeenshire are rich lands, both for crops and in fish. In the middle ages at least, salmon was one of Aberdeen's exports.[13] The Mearns, Angus and Fife continue the same mixture of good land and river valleys. And from here the North Sea provides a channel to the markets of the Netherlands, already by the end of the twelfth century the most advanced economy in northern Europe. Development needs both resources on the spot and contact with potential markets where primary products can be traded for luxuries. It was on this eastern coast that many of the major towns of medieval Scotland developed – most notably Aberdeen, Dundee and Perth. These would never rival the metropolises of the medieval economy – London, Bruges, Ghent, or the Hanseatic towns – indeed John Barbour, writing in the 1370s, could, in a speech attributed to a French visitor, describe

Perth as 'ane wretchit hamlet'[14] – but by Scottish standards, and indeed probably by the standards of Norway, these were substantial places, probably rivalling all but Bergen in the north. Along with Berwick, they were the main centres of early medieval Scottish trade.

The picture, and the external contacts, change again south of the Forth. South-eastern Scotland divides into two parts: Lothian itself – the land to the north of the Lammermuirs and Pentlands; and the Borders – the complex network of valleys centring on Tweed and Teviot, the lands of the Border Abbeys, and much later of Sir Walter Scott. Lothian is a rich agricultural area, whose wealth clearly encouraged the development of Edinburgh, the natural fortress which dominates the area, and the site of an abbey. It is not surprising that Edinburgh was to become the capital: its castle and abbey must themselves have provided a source of income for the inhabitants of the two burghs that developed: Edinburgh itself, which grew up to the south and east of the castle around the High Street and the Grassmarket; and the Canongate, the burgh of the Augustinian canons of Holyrood, at the lower end of what is now known as the 'Royal Mile'. Edinburgh's structure and position suggests that, unlike the other towns so far mentioned, it was essentially a service town, meeting the needs of castle and abbey. Its rise to prominence in the fourteenth century depended on two things: the loss of Berwick to the English, first in 1296 and again in 1333 (much of its trade had to be transferred to Edinburgh's port of Leith); and the fact that from David II's reign onwards Edinburgh became effectively the centre of government. By the end of the middle ages, it had far outstripped all other Scottish towns.

The wealth of the Borders was quite different. In its lower reaches the Tweed valley opens out into the lands known as the Merse, rich until Anglo-Scottish war subjected them to constant raiding in the fourteenth century and beyond. The rivers were also rich in fish, especially salmon, and in Berwick the area possessed what was till 1296 certainly the premier port and burgh in Scotland. The wealth of the area depended overwhelmingly on the four great abbeys, founded in the twelfth century, whose lands became the great sheep farms of medieval Scotland. The Borders became, after the south of England, the chief producer of wool in western Europe, ultimately for the Flemish cloth industry. Berwick's wealth depended on its position as the chief exporter of Scottish wool, a trade which was gradually but substantially transferred to Leith in the fourteenth century. Berwick had attracted English settlers as well as merchants from the continent; and the economy of the Borders was more closely linked to England than that of any other part of Scotland. The region's ultimate fierce Scottishness was a product of the conflicts which stretch from 1296 to 1603.

What is striking, however, as we survey the elements of development that existed is that these elements in no way helped to tie Scotland together. Scotland's trade, its contacts with the more developed economies of the south-western seas, of Scandinavia, of the Netherlands, and of the Baltic, were as diverse as the physical structure of the country. The various areas we have looked at were all linked with quite distinct economic areas. Just as there was no obvious geographical centre to Scotland, no natural link between the diverse geographical regions, so there was no economic centre, no London at once the dominant centre of trade and government, to make Scotland one. The economics of the different regions pulled them, if it were possible, further apart.

There is no answer here to the problem of the source of a Scottish identity.

2

THE IDENTITY OF ORDER

As we have seen, the root of what was to be the Scottish kingdom was in the union of Picts and Scots in the ninth century to form the kingdom of Alba. But there was still a long way to go. Alba covered only the territories between the Forth/Clyde isthmus and the Great Glen. To the north, lay Moray – the lands round the Moray Firth, and including much of what is now Wester Ross – which was much involved with Alba, but for long not exactly part of it. The north and west, now Caithness, Sutherland and the Western and Northern Isles, were controlled by Scandinavian settlers, only loosely and nominally governed by the kings of Norway. South of the Forth/Clyde isthmus, there was still Strathclyde under its own rulers in the west, and the region of Lothian in the east, dominated by an Anglian aristocracy much connected with Northumbria.

Nevertheless, the kingdom of Alba was to last, and prove a solid base for expansion. Its kings were the most powerful in what was ultimately to be Scotland; and both Strathclyde and Lothian needed support at times against Norse settlements in Cumbria and against the Danish kingdom of York, while it lasted (till 954); and subsequently against the threat of expanding Wessex. The kings of Alba, in such a situation, were a force to be reckoned with. They could intervene in the affairs of southern Britain, as Constantine II did in 937, when

21

he joined the coalition of the Norse and perhaps Strathclyde, a coalition which was decisively defeated by Athelstan of Wessex, at the battle of Brunanburh. Curiously, the result seems to have been a tightening of the authority of Alba, as Athelstan's successors increased their grip on the north of England. Those parts not falling under the English power, Strathclyde and Lothian, became more firmly client states of Alba.[1] By the end of the tenth century, though there was still a 'king' of Strathclyde (or perhaps 'under-king'), Alba was dominant over both.

Its kings had, however, both to maintain their influence over the southern areas – which were neither Scottish nor Pictish, but alien in language, race and history – and to hold their own against the Norse in Orkney and Caithness. Effectively independent of Norway, the Norse power reached its zenith in the rule of Earl Thorfinn the Mighty, who died some time in the 1050s or early 1060s. These challenges seemed to have had some effect on the internal structures of Alba. At the beginning of the tenth century, when the recently united kingdom was trying to cope with the rising Scandinavian threat which followed the establishment of the earldom of Orkney in the late ninth century,[2] the rank of *mormaer* appears. The title means 'great steward' and is used for the rulers of Moray, Strathearn, Buchan, Angus and Mearns. These are just the areas where there would be a need for an efficient militia as a result of the Viking threat.[3] The new 'provinces' seem strikingly like Ottonian 'marches'; at the time an advance in authority, yet also in the future a potential threat. The defender of the frontiers could easily turn into a challenge to the ruler.

In fact, the history of Scottish kingship from the eleventh century to the thirteenth is a mixture of consolidation and internal challenges. The client states of Strathclyde and Lothian were to remain subject to the kings of *Scotia*, 'Scotland', as by the eleventh century the kingdom of Alba was coming to be known; though the term *Scotia*, like Alba, did not yet cover the areas to the south of the Forth and Clyde isthmus. The last appearance, apparently, of a king of Strathclyde was in the army of Malcolm II of Scots at the battle fought at Carham on the Tweed against Earl Uhtred of Bamburgh, in 1016 or 1018. The power of Scotia to the north and west was much less secure. The Western Isles, the northern mainland, and Orkney and Shetland were Norse. The proximity of these Norse areas meant that Scotia had little effective power over the western mainland; and the area to north and west of the Great Glen remained problematic. The men of Moray, an ill-defined area which may have stretched from the hills of Strathbogie as far west as the sea at Kyle of Lochalsh, were a recurrent problem. One of their rulers, Macbeth, was able from 1040 till at least 1054 to displace the main lines of the kings of Alba/Scotia; and subsequent revolts continued until the early thirteenth century. Nevertheless, by the middle of the eleventh century, the kingdom of Alba/Scotia had existed for over two hundred years and showed every sign of continuing.

What did the authority of its kings amount to? The kings of Alba/Scotia, like kings everywhere in western Europe in these centuries, were essentially war-leaders. We know little of them save the battles that they fought, for that was all the sketchy chronicles of the time tell us, along with the bald listing of their successions. From the king-lists, it is evident that the kings of Alba were all related, but they did not come from a single line: collaterals, members of any branch of the royal line, might succeed; and disputes over the succession were common.[4] Even Macbeth could claim descent from one of the early royal kin groups, the Cenél Loairn, and his wife was a granddaughter of Kenneth III, king from 996 to 1005. Macbeth was finally overthrown in 1057 by Malcolm Canmore, the son of the Duncan I whom Macbeth had displaced in 1040. Malcolm's recovery of the throne, with the help of northern–English relatives, especially Siward, Earl of Northumbria, was in two stages, a reflection perhaps of the divisions in the territory that was subject to the kings of Scotia. In 1054 Malcolm recovered the southern part of the country –

we are not certain exactly how much. Macbeth seems to have retired over the Mounth, perhaps retreating towards his original territory of Moray. He was eventually killed three years later, in 1057, at Lumphanan in the south of Aberdeenshire. His stepson Lulach, himself a member of the kin of Alpin, was enthroned as king as a rival to Malcolm, but was in turn killed, early in 1058, at Essie, near Rhynie in the north-east of Aberdeenshire, close to the border of Moray. The mac Alpin kin was thus restored, if by stages, to the rule of Alba/Scotia; but the succession was still open to challenge from different lines within the kin. When Malcolm Canmore (Malcolm III) was killed in battle in 1093, the succession was disputed between Donald bàn, Malcolm's brother, and Duncan, son of Malcolm by his first wife Ingibiorg, the widow, or perhaps the daughter of Earl Thorfinn of Orkney.[5] Not until 1097 was another of Malcolm's sons, Edgar, placed on the throne with the support of William II Rufus, king of England. He was the son of Malcolm's second wife, Margaret, granddaughter of the Edmund Ironside who had briefly ruled England in 1016 before his defeat by the Danish invader Cnut. This established in Scotland a dynasty, variously known to historians as the Canmore dynasty or the mac Malcolm dynasty, which was to hold the throne in the main line until the death of Alexander III in 1286. The year 1097 therefore marked a fundamental change in the successional structure of the Scottish kingdom, away from collateral succession.

Much the same had happened a century earlier in France. There, from the late ninth century, various rival lines had disputed the succession, often from different territorial bases, until the election in 987 of Hugh Capet, a descendant of Robert the Strong, count of the Breton march in the mid-ninth century. From then on, good luck and a certain amount of contrivance enabled the Capetians to maintain the succession in the male line until 1328. This long succession had a fundamental effect on the sense of identity of the peoples under their rule, which could never have been given by the shifting lines of the previous century.

In the eleventh century, however, kings anywhere had few means to assert direct authority: most depended heavily on the men who held local power, often themselves as war-leaders and self-made families. The best the kings could do was attempt to bind these local powers to themselves by oaths of vassalage, promises to stand by the king in time of need, promises whose performance usually depended on timely and forceful pressure, in so far as the kings had the means to apply it. Their authority also depended on the capacity of the kings to support their vassals, when these vassals in turn needed it. Otherwise, kings depended on the power given by the lands they held directly, and on the influence they could exert over the church and its lands, for the church always looked to kings as its protectors against predatory local barons, and hence was one of the main supports of royal power. That support again depended on the kings' being able to provide effective protection when it was needed. At every turn, kings had to be successful war leaders. Weakness in war meant disaster.

However, the nature of government was changing in the twelfth century. The development of education outside monasteries, in the cathedral schools which were ultimately to become the universities of the middle ages, made available a supply of literate clerks who could operate systems depending on written orders and eventually on written records. Thomas Becket, chancellor to the English king Henry II before he became archbishop, is the most famous British example of a royal servant trained in the schools. English government as it was to develop in the twelfth century depended on many such. A few of these literate clerks wrote accounts of the systems they administered, which let us understand something of the new style of government. Ranulf Glanville, for example, wrote a treatise on the working of English law during the reign of Henry II, which is our main guide to that king's reforms in justice.

The structures varied very much in different kingdoms, depending on the history and styles of government which had developed over centuries. France was an example of a feudal state, where the great lords had dominated wide territories; and where royal administration, as it developed quite late in the twelfth century, worked by elaborating royal means of control over the feudatories, a process which proved far from easy, since the kings had relatively little land under their direct control. The much smaller state of the counts of Flanders could be much more centralised, for in various ways the counts controlled much more of the land, through territories they had acquired themselves, or through their control of church lands gained in the ninth and tenth centuries, when the church was much weakened by Viking raids. Their authority could be exercised through the castellans of the castles which the counts established on their lands, castellans who acted as the counts' local agents.[6]

England followed a pattern of its own. The conquest of the regions of Scandinavian settlement in the tenth century by the kings of Wessex had spread a system of local territorial government over most of the country. This created an organisation of counties, administered nominally by earls, but effectively by the king's reeves, who presided over the county courts, formally as deputies of the earls. The Latin term for an earl was *comes*, from which was derived the county, *comitatus*. The king's reeve, who became the shire reeve (*scir gerefa*) or sheriff, was in Latin the *vicecomes*, literally vice-earl. In England, there was a system of local government under royal control, which was hardly paralleled elsewhere.

Scotland, however, was ill-suited physically for any kind of centralised administration; nor was she in any sense a feudal state at the time when Malcolm III finally overthrew Macbeth in 1057. She was a still state of many peoples, each with their own 'kings' or 'under-kings' or 'lords'. One of the main problems of Malcolm and his successors was to establish their authority over these regional kings or under-kings. In such a situation, royal authority was not going to be easy to develop. Yet as we have seen, the kings of Scots were recognised as lords over a wide area; and they were given the precious asset of time to develop their position.

Surprisingly, it was to be support from the neighbouring English which proved crucial in establishing the succession of Malcolm's dynasty, and in upholding and increasing its authority. Malcolm III's connections with England, where he had spent the greater part of Macbeth's reign with the support of his relative Earl Siward of Northumbria, and also, it seems, with the backing of the English king, Edward the Confessor, began a time of useful contacts which were to help his descendants in their efforts to strengthen their position within Scotland.

After Edward the Confessor's death in 1065, and the conquest of England by the Norman Duke William in 1066, Malcolm provided a refuge for Edgar Ætheling, the grandson of the Edmund Ironside who had been displaced by the Danish invader Cnut in 1016; and with Edgar came his sister Margaret, whom, around 1070, Malcolm married as his second wife. Not surprisingly, Malcolm gave aid to a number of rebels against William, as a result of which William marched into Scotland in 1072 and compelled Malcolm to give hostages for good behaviour and become his vassal, though, according to the Anglo-Saxon Chronicle, William 'gained no advantage' from this expedition.[7] In fact, throughout his reign, Malcolm invaded England five times in all, and seems to have ignored whatever obligations he conceived he owed as a vassal. But his interventions, and his connections with the previous English monarchy, made him a power the Norman kings needed to reckon with, in days when their own authority was insecure.

Paradoxically, these conflicts opened up what were to be very fruitful contacts for Malcolm's descendants. In the conflicts after Malcolm's death referred to earlier between his brother Donald bàn and his son Duncan by his first marriage, it was English support for the house of Canmore which was to prove decisive. Duncan had been in England as a hostage ever since the 'settlement' of 1072, and had stayed there voluntarily after William the Conqueror's death in 1087, although released from captivity by William Rufus, who succeeded the Conqueror. Edgar Ætheling, who had pursued a very complex path of successive submissions to and revolts against William the Conqueror, seems to have made a lasting peace with William Rufus, and from then on appears to have acted as an elder statesman on behalf of his Scottish relatives.

Since Duncan, Malcolm's son, was still in England, it was perhaps natural that, on Malcolm's death in 1093, 'the Scots elected Donald, Malcolm's brother as king, and [according to the Anglo-Saxon Chronicle] drove out all the English who had been with king Malcolm'.[8] These English were presumably descendants of the exiles of 1066, but we have no certain knowledge.

However, with Duncan and Edgar Ætheling at Rufus' court, help was at hand for the children of king Malcolm. Duncan with Rufus' consent and 'such English and French assistance as he could obtain … deprived Donald his kinsman of the kingdom and was received as king'.[9] This English intervention did not last long: in 1094 'the Scots entrapped and slew Duncan, their king, and thereafter for the second time took Donald, his paternal uncle, to be their king, by whose counsel and instigation he [Duncan] was betrayed to his death'.[10] These events are open to many interpretations, most obviously as a 'Scottish' reaction against 'English' influences; though also as the kind of struggle within the royal kin which had long been characteristic of Scottish and other monarchies.

However we should interpret these events, and there is no native Scottish account to guide us, they provoked a response from Malcolm's second family. It seems that, during Donald's reign, several of the sons of Malcolm Canmore and Margaret took refuge with their uncle, Edgar Ætheling, in England; and in 1097, it was again with Rufus' support that the eldest of these exiles, also called Edgar, was installed by Edgar Ætheling as king, Donald being imprisoned and apparently slain, perhaps much later, in captivity. It was with English help that the Canmore dynasty was established, and it was to rule Scotland till 1286.

These events established what were to be very important connections between the mac Malcolm dynasty and the Anglo-

Norman nobility. Malcolm Canmore himself and at least his
son Edgar, as we have seen, depended on English support to
establish themselves; and Malcolm is said to have introduced
Englishmen to Scotland, presumably as settlers or courtiers,
perhaps 'household knights' like those of the Norman kings
of England. We have no details. David I, who succeeded to the
throne in 1124, had spent much of the early years of
the twelfth century as an English baron. He already possessed vassals in his English earldoms of Huntingdon and
Northampton, men whom he knew and could trust. When he
wanted to establish his authority in Scotland, it was natural
that he should see the advantages of giving these men landed
positions in his realm. Renfrewshire he gave to Walter son of
Alan, a junior member of what was to become the fitzAlan
family in England. In Scotland, they were to take their name
from the hereditary office they held at David's court, the
office of Steward, though it is not till the fourteenth century
that the name Stewart clearly appears as a surname. Hugh de
Morville, descended from a knightly family in the Cotentin
and probably a younger son of a family which was steadily
rising in Anglo-Norman England, became a member of
David's circle in the earldom of Northampton, and later
became his Constable in Scotland. He was given Kyle in
Ayrshire and Lauder on the southern fringe of the
Lammermuirs. Ranulph de Soules, the Butler, was given
Liddesdale; and Robert Bruce, Lord of Brix in the Cotentin
and Cleveland in North Yorkshire, was granted Annandale in
one of David's earliest surviving charters.[11] These were only
the greatest of a substantial number of grants which David
made to Anglo-Norman barons. The lands were all held by
feudal tenures, which seem to have been introduced to
Scotland at this point; and which were copied by David's two
successors, his grandsons Malcolm IV, king from 1153 to 1165,
and William I, often later called William the Lion, who ruled
from 1165 to 1214. Under them, feudal tenures extended as
far as Aberdeenshire, Buchan and the Laich of Moray. But the
territorial implications of these grants are surely more

significant than the tenurial. By the middle of David I's reign, much of southern Scotland was in the hands of Anglo-Norman companions of the king who showed themselves loyal and determined to uphold his authority. They were often accompanied by followers who were in turn given estates by the principal landholders.[12]

How this was possible is a difficult question which has been carefully examined by Professor Barrow in the second chapter of his *Anglo-Norman Era in Scottish History*. The basis of the grants was probably the demesne lands of the crown; most were in areas already settled and, after a complex analysis of place-names, Professor Barrow suggests that 'we have the impression of a country' (before the Anglo-Norman settlement) 'far from depopulated, but settled loosely and extensively enough for newcomers to enter by royal favour and practise a more extensive exploitation of resources'.[13] Some of the valuations given in the Domesday survey of England suggest that the Normans to whom William the Conqueror granted lands were able to exact, perhaps even extort, considerably more than had their English predecessors; there was perhaps scope for the Anglo-Norman settlers in twelfth-century Scotland to do likewise.

These settlers gave David I and his successors a body of supporters who owed their position to the crown and who, at least for a generation or two, would maintain royal authority against regional opposition. But there were also developments in the institutions of government which strengthened the authority of the kings and brought Scotland more into line with what was happening elsewhere in western Europe, even if the structures and institutions in Scotland took forms which reflected the particular nature of the country and its societies.

David I introduced sheriffs to Scotland, an office clearly derived from England where the English sheriffs were descended from the king's reeves who appear as royal officials in late Anglo-Saxon times, when the 'earls' were great potentates, ruling several shires. The *scir gerefa*, the 'shire reeve', later the sheriff, had become the king's principal officer in the county. In Scotland, the sheriffs introduced by David I were called *vicecomites*, like the English sheriffs, but they had no relationship, even nominal, to the Scottish earls. The first sheriff appears at Roxburgh in the 1120s before David became king, and others are soon recorded at Scone, Berwick, Stirling, Clackmannan, Perth, and Aberdeen and Banff (the last jointly).[14] They were, however, given charge, not of counties, but of sheriffdoms, *vicecomitatus*. The unit was as much a new creation as the office and took its name from the officer. ('Counties' did not appear in Scotland until 1889, when county councils were created in Scotland on the model of the English ones established in 1888.)

Although the title of sheriff was derived from England, the office and the unit were adapted to the very different and less centralised structures in Scotland. They were much more like the castellans and castellanries of early medieval Flanders where, as we have seen, the counts of the tenth to twelfth centuries built comital castles at important sites in their country – the best known today is at Ghent where a castle of perhaps the tenth century was later replaced by the imposing 'Castle of the Counts of Flanders' which still impresses tourists; the counts entrusted the government of parts of their county to the castellans of these castles which served as strong points from which to maintain their authority over the surrounding area. Professor Dickinson long ago demonstrated that royal castles were the central feature of most sheriffdoms.[15] The Scottish sheriff, however, was and has remained in Scotland to this day, much more a judge that his counterparts in England, whose jurisdiction was quickly circumscribed by the emergence of central royal courts in the late twelfth century. In Scotland, professional royal judges had hardly developed by the end of the middle ages and justice remained far more in the hands of sheriffs and regional justiciars, invariably barons, who handled much of the business which in England was the province of itinerant, increasingly professional, royal justices.[16] The writs (in Scotland *brieves*) which developed in the twelfth and thirteenth

31

centuries, reflected the difference between the two systems. The English writ of novel disseisin, issued in cases where a plaintiff claimed to have been wrongfully dispossessed of his land, was an order to the sheriff to take sureties from the parties, to restore possession to the claimant for the time being, to empanel a jury to view the disputed land, and produce all of the parties before the king's justices who would decide the case when they came round to the county on their eyres.[17] The sheriff was simply an agent serving the needs of a more centralised system. His own direct jurisdiction was far more limited and less important, leaving him as the chief official in local administration. In Scotland, the equivalent of the writ of novel disseisin, the brieve *de nova dissaisina* was an order to the justiciars to try the case.[18] The intention was that justice should be handled, as far as possible, in the localities. Scotland saw much less than England of the blending of local communities and royal centralisation.

Royal finance, too, was much less centralised than in England. Royal revenues, as in England, derived partly from royal lands, which were administered by the sheriffs, and partly from tolls and customs, collected by burgh officials. In both countries, much royal expenditure was incurred directly in the localities and was paid out by local officials without ever being paid in to central coffers. Scotland, however, had nothing like the English Exchequer, which operated as a central financial institution, receiving revenues, paying out moneys due from the crown, auditing accounts of office-holders at all levels and sitting also as a court with jurisdiction over all financial matters. There were in Scotland sessions of 'auditors of accounts' whose sittings were recorded in rolls of accounts, which survive as originals from the late 1320s (a few copies of texts from the 1260s have been preserved); but these officials were specially appointed to audit the accounts and are so described in the records. From the 1330s, these sessions of audit are sometimes described as 'The Exchequer' (*Scaccarium*), but the auditors did not constitute a permanent institution and they did not receive money.[19] Money, in so far as it was not expended locally, was handled by the Chamberlain and his clerks, who were, as in England, household officials, whose accounts, in so far as they survive among the rolls, give us our only information on the central finances of the kingdom.

The central institutions that existed in medieval Scotland were essentially household institutions. At least until well on in the fifteenth century, central Scottish government was household government, in the hands of the king himself and his immediate household officials. The Chancellor kept the Great Seal; from the late thirteenth century, there was a privy or secret seal (as yet the terms were interchangeable) which in the 1360s seems to have been in the charge of the kings secretary;[20] but the documents to be sealed were normally produced by the clerks of the king's chapel, rather than in a separate chancery; and there are some cases where it looks as though the scribes were either clerks of the recipients or belonged to abbeys where the king was when the charters were granted, rather than being regular royal clerks.[21] This is reminiscent of late Anglo-Saxon England rather than any later period; though occasional English royal charters were still being written by recipients in the fourteenth century.

Because central government in medieval Scotland was on a small scale, run by a few clerks and clerical and baronial officials, there were none of the sort of offices which produced and kept the masses of records which are the basis of so much medieval English history. The better comparison is between the records of medieval government in Scotland and the records of the medieval English royal household. The problem, however, is not that the Scottish kings did not keep records in the period before 1286, but that almost all the early records disappeared at the time of the interregnum at the end of the thirteenth century. We know from an inventory of 1292 that there were then in Edinburgh castle a total of almost 800 rolls and a large number of individual documents. Some at least of these items dated from the twelfth century.[22]

None of this means that medieval Scottish government was either inefficient or primitive; just that it grew up in a country very differently structured from medieval England, where the localities dominated government far more than they did in England. No medieval government anywhere in Europe was centralised in the way that the governments of Louis XIV, or Frederick II of Prussia or the Czars of Russia were in later centuries. Everywhere, kings had to rule through local powers, magnates and communities; but in Scotland, as in France and Germany, the balance was tipped far more towards the localities than it was in England. It may have been England that was exceptional rather than Scotland.

Apart from strictly governmental forms, other aspects of Scottish life were changing in the twelfth century in ways which often increased the authority of the kings. As we shall see in chapter 3, both Queen Margaret, Malcolm Canmore's second wife, and David I were anxious to bring the Scottish church more into line with the norms established in western Europe. Though the conversion of Scotland had begun as early as the sixth and seventh centuries, the patterns then established had been those of a Celtic monastic church, but one which never experienced either the elaborate monastic reforms of the Carolingian era and later centuries; nor had it yet acquired a formal diocesan organisation. Both aspects were taken up by Margaret and by two of her sons, Alexander I, who reigned from 1107 to 1124, and David I, king from 1124 to 1153. By the end of David's reign, Scotland had both a thriving group of monasteries, most belonging to the latest reformed orders; and a well-developed diocesan system, covering at least the area from the Borders to the Great Glen. The motives of these kings were surely religious but, as elsewhere, the church could be a formidable support to royal authority, since it was to the crown that the church always looked for protection. Monasteries were important landowners; bishops were men of education and served often as officials in royal government. Without the church, most of the developments in royal government would have been impossible.

David I also seems to have been concerned to develop the economy of his country. He was the first king whom we know to have struck a Scottish coinage. Evidence for the development of towns is limited: but in the laws attributed to David I, there are regulations for the affairs of the 'Four Burghs', Edinburgh, Roxburgh, Berwick and Stirling. Presumably, these centres were natural growths: all were on natural sites for the development of towns; but from David's reign, we have examples of other burghs to which the king had granted trading and market privileges in return for tolls, generally following English models; they were often colonised by English and continental settlers.[23] Fifteen places can be listed which certainly existed as royal burghs by the end of David I's reign in 1153, including Elgin, Forres and Aberdeen in the north-east.[24] These were all centres of royal influence, often in areas where this was very valuable to the crown. As in other countries, we have to guess at the origin of these towns: probably a mixture of natural growth at suitable sites, with the deliberate encouragement of royal privileges.

By the early thirteenth century, the kings of Scots had established their authority in what we can conceive as a series of regions with their centre at St Andrews, in some sense by that time the spiritual centre of the kingdom. In Angus, Fife, Lothian and the districts around the towns of Perth and Stirling, an area which became by the twelfth century the heartland of the Scottish monarchy, the kings had direct authority; these were economically the most advanced parts of the country where farming land was good, where lay many of the new burghs founded by twelfth-century kings and where merchants could trade across the North Sea and bring in tolls to the crown.

Elsewhere, royal authority had to depend on local powers, but in various ways the kings were able to bind those powers to themselves, so that even indirectly the royal power was a force and so a factor in creating an identity. We must look in turn at the different regions to see how this was done.

Royal power in the eastern and central Borders south of the Lammermuirs was greatly enhanced when David I, even before he became king, founded the Abbey of Selkirk around 1113 (the site proved unsuitable and the house was soon moved to the more open site of Kelso); to be followed by Melrose in 1136 and Jedburgh a few years later. Abbeys were great landholders, endowed not only by their founders but by many others in the neighbourhood; like ecclesiastical landholders everywhere in western Europe, they rallied for their own protection to the crown whose support they always needed. There was good political sense as well as piety in David's foundations: the Border abbeys created an area of royal influence in the valleys of the Tweed and its tributaries which lasted till the Wars of Independence. It was an area which the kings visited frequently. Effective authority required the king's personal presence; and we can gauge the areas in which their influence was strongest from the places in which kings issued charters and other documents. In the late twelfth and early thirteenth centuries, the bulk of William the Lion's sealed documents (technically described as 'acts') were issued in Forfar, Fife, Kinross, Lothian and at Stirling, Clackmannan and Perth; no less than 322 'acts' were issued in the inner area of royal authority. Elsewhere, there were only a handful, twenty-eight in the north-east, fifteen in the Clyde valley, three in Dumfriesshire, but no less than 110 in the Tweed valley and the valleys of its tributaries. The pattern shows very clearly the limits of royal authority; and also the importance of the new Border foundations: 61 'acts' were issued at Melrose, Jedburgh, Selkirk and Roxburgh in the heart of the abbey country.[25]

Outside these areas, the kings had to depend on others, notably on those who held the great fiefs given by David I to his Anglo-Norman companions, fiefs which extended over Renfrewshire, Kyle in Ayrshire, Annandale in Dumfriesshire, Lauderdale on the southern fringe of the Lammermuirs, filling the gap between Lothian and the area of the Border abbeys, and Eskdale and Liddesdale in the western Borders. By the middle of David I's reign, much of southern Scotland outside the inner circle of royal authority had as feudal superiors the Anglo-Norman followers of the king who showed themselves loyal and determined to uphold his authority. These grants carried royal authority, albeit indirectly, into areas where it must previously have been much more tenuous.

Beyond these regions, there was yet another situation, in some sense beyond the range of direct royal authority altogether: a great swath of territory stretching from Galloway in the south-west through Menteith and Strathearn to Moray in the north and including also the Western Isles, Argyll, Ross and Caithness, Orkney and Shetland, the outermost region of all. These areas had identities and authorities of their own, many with ancient traditions behind them, and often with foreign links to bolster their individuality. Galloway, and Argyll and the Isles, were inextricably involved in the affairs of Man and Ireland, and mainly looked after their own affairs in the twelfth century with minimal interference from the kings of Scots. The far north and the Hebrides continued to be a region of Norse principalities which kings of Norway from Magnus Barelegs at the end of the eleventh century to Haakon Haakonson in the thirteenth occasionally tried to bring under control. Menteith and Strathearn seem largely to have escaped Anglo-Norman settlement, perhaps because they were less economically attractive and less strategically important than the lands to the south and east which were such a rich field for exploitation by the newcomers; while Moray was a great territory stretching in early days from the Laich of Moray on the coast of the Moray Firth to Wester Ross.

Moray proved to be a power which the kings of Scots found they had to confront. Its ruler in the mid-eleventh century was Macbeth, whose wife was a member of the royal kin of Alba, and who was able in 1040 to overthrow Duncan I and make himself king of Alba. Though the dynasty of Duncan was restored in 1054–7, Moray remained a recurrent threat.

Macbeth's stepson Lulach maintained his claim to the kingdom, presumably in the right of his mother (he was her son by her first marriage) for a few months after Macbeth's death. His son, Malsnechtai, was defeated by Malcolm III in 1078 but is still described as 'king' of Moray (the Irish term would cover 'under-king') in the Annals of Ulster at the time of his death in 1085.[26] In 1130 there was a 'rebellion' by Angus, Earl of Moray, and one Malcolm mac Heth who seems to have had an obscure claim both to the earldom and the kingdom. The rebellion was defeated and Angus killed; Malcolm mac Heth was captured in 1134 and imprisoned in Roxburgh, from which he was not released until 1157, probably as part of a complex attempted pacification, involving Argyll and the Isles as well.[27] The defeat of the men of Moray in 1130 was seen by contemporaries as a decisive event: the Chronicle of Melrose says that 'Angus earl of Moray was killed with his people by the Scots.' The Annals of Ulster refer to 'a battle between the men of Scotland and the men of Moray' in which 'four thousand of the men of Moray fell, including their king Angus'.[28] These accounts clearly see Moray as a distinct indentity, on a par with and opposed to Scotland. David I seems to have been determined to get a grip on the area and used all the resources he could muster to that end. By 1124 there was a bishop of Moray, who, being appointed by the king, could represent royal as well as ecclesiastical authority. The Priory of Urquhart was founded around 1136 and the Abbey of Kinloss in 1150. After the 'revolt' of 1130, a Fleming, Freskin, already settled in Lothian was given the estate of Duffus, near Elgin in Moray, and became the leader of a significant Flemish settlement and the ancestor of the great family of *de Moravia* (Moray or Murray);[29] burghs existed at Forres and Elgin before 1153.[30] The whole gamut of David's new institutions was put in place; yet despite all the burghs, religious houses and Flemish settlers, Moray remained a centre of trouble: in 1163 there is a strange reference in the Holyrood Chronicle to 'the removal of the men of Moray',[31] a curt reference to what may have been an early example of 'ethnic cleansing' though that has been disputed. It certainly has no known context. In the late twelfth and early thirteenth centuries there was a series of rebellions in Moray headed by, among others, Donald mac William and his son Guthred, the descendants, possibly illegitimate, of William, a son of Duncan II. These rebellions forced William the Lion to repeated campaigns in the north from 1179 until 1212 and to the building of royal castles at Redcastle and Dunskeath in Moray.[32] Moray clearly preserved its identity and hostility towards the kings of Scots until well into the thirteenth century. Another revolt had to be suppressed in 1215, at the very beginning of the reign of William the Lion's son, Alexander II.

Elsewhere, tactics had to be adapted to circumstances: kings of Scots had to be opportunists and make use of what support they could gain. It was a tactic which often preserved local identities but tried to exploit them in the kings' interests. The situation on the western seaboard is a good example. Here there were two external forces, Scandinavian and Manx. The Scandinavian settlements in the Isles were intermittently subject to the kings of Norway, who for long period were too preoccupied with troubles at home to take much interest in them. They therefore fell under the dominance of whatever local powers could prevail, usually the Norse jarls who were based in Orkney. The 'kingdom' of Man, however, also at times claimed authority over much of the Inner Hebrides. In the early twelfth century, there developed two other local powers in this area, both of obscure origin: Somerled, whose authority stretched from Kintyre to Mull and included a certain amount of the mainland; and Fergus, who is described as 'lord', occasionally 'king' in Irish sources, of Galloway. These two were, as far as we can tell, independent both of David I and of the Norse and Manx; but there is some reason to believe that David I helped to build up the authority of Somerled, with whom he seems to have been on good terms.[33] Somerled's rise was perhaps a move towards a 'Scottish' as distinct from a Scandinavian authority in the west, at least on the mainland and in the inner isles; and was probably the best the Scottish kings could do to achieve some influence in a fiercely independent area.

A similar policy was developed in Galloway, where Fergus may also have been backed by David I. However, Malcolm IV, David I's grandson, who succeeded as king in 1153 at the age of about twelve, is described as having 'subdued' the area in campaigns in 1160, after a revolt in which Fergus was involved.[34] After Fergus's death in 1161, Galloway was torn by conflicts between his sons, Uhtred and Gilbert (born of different mothers), conflicts which culminated in Gilbert's murder of Uhtred in 1174. Ultimately, Uhtred's son Roland recovered his father's lands, perhaps as part of a settlement in 1176 or 1178 overseen by Henry II, who was taking seriously the overlordship of Scotland which he had exacted in the Treaty of Falaise in 1174 (for which see below, pp. 43–4). There was renewed conflict in the 1180s and after Gilbert's death in 1185, Roland seized the remainder of the lordship of Galloway. This led to a conflict between Roland and Gilbert's son, which gave Henry II another opportunity to intervene in Scotland and impose a settlement over the head of a seemingly reluctant William the Lion, a settlement which involved William in giving compensation to Gilbert's son, in the form of the lordship, later the earldom, of Carrick.[35] Roland then joined William in the campaign in the north in 1187, which overthrew the rebel Donald mac William.[36] The result in this case of Henry's intervention was to gain for the King of Scots two loyal supporters in Galloway and Carrick who would back the king in return for their own authority in their territories remaining unchallenged. The earls of Menteith and Strathearn were probably also left to themselves, with only nominal control by the king provided they remained loyal: there were few settlements of 'feudal' barons in these latter areas; in Galloway, on the other hand, where the kings had to assert their authority more openly, there is evidence of some feudal settlements of outsiders, especially in the third quarter of the century, the period of the disputes between Uhtred and Gilbert.[37]

Scotland, by the thirteenth century, was a kingdom of many parts and many identities; yet it was clearly a single kingdom. The revolts which caused so much trouble to the kings, particularly in the twelfth century, underlined the elements of regional particularism, but, given the loose traditions of succession in earlier centuries and the number of lines which could trace their descent to Duncan I, they are hardly surprising. A similar plethora of descendants of Edward III in England is often credited with some part in generating the conflicts known as the Wars of the Roses. What is remarkable in Scotland is how determinedly the main line was preserved. The revolts were mostly conflicts within the very wide royal kin, conflicts which expressed local opposition or the sense of regional particularism, rather than being attempts to overthrow the kings, whose position was never seriously challenged.

As we have seen, however, many of the changes which took place in the twelfth century had depended on, and served to strengthen, links with England. The 'Norman' settlers, whatever their ultimate origins, nearly all came immediately from England and were men whom David I had known during his years at the English court before he became king in 1124. His monasteries were mostly founded from mother houses in England; some at least of the leading Scottish churchmen were of English origin (see Chapter 6 below). This close relationship with the English crown and the English nobility in the twelfth century gave rise to two sets of problems. Firstly, English links were not always popular in Scotland, and could cause trouble within the country; and secondly, the connections with England could establish a sense of Scotland's being dependent on its southern neighbour, which could encourage the tendency of the kings of England to see themselves as, in some sense, overlords of Scotland. This tendency might, in the long run, threaten the independence and even the identity of the country.

We have already noted the references in the Anglo-Saxon Chronicle to the Scots ejecting English after the death of Malcolm Canmore in 1093; and to the slaughter in the following year of the followers of Duncan II, who were, on the Chronicle's account, English and French.[38] The recurrent troubles with Moray, which continued into the reign of David I and beyond, may also have been in part an expression of hostility to David's reforms and to the Anglo-Normans and Frenchmen he trusted. The kings' own close connections with England also caused some discontent at times. There was enthusiasm for invading England in 1138, when David I supported his niece, the Empress Matilda, daughter of Henry I, in the English civil war against King Stephen, even though the Battle of the Standard in that year proved a disastrous defeat for the Scots. On the other hand, there was much hostility to the king of Scots leaving Britain in support of Henry II's campaign in Toulouse in 1159, in the course of which he was knighted by the English king. On Malcolm's return he was faced with, and defeated, a very serious rising of six Scottish earls, which may have been an expression of protest.[39] Even William the Lion was apparently criticised in the early thirteenth century for being more 'French' (i.e. perhaps Norman) than Scots.[40] The comment was admittedly made by an English source, the Barnwell Annalist, but may well reflect Scottish feelings.

Some hostility was natural to Anglo-Norman interlopers, who were in effect a new layer in the political structures, and who must have taken their toll of resources; and also to kings who were too much involved in English affairs; but there were many other factors involved in the complex politics of Scotland in the eleventh and twelfth centuries. Anti-foreign feelings were certainly there at times; but so was a long tradition of regional independence which saw the kings of Alba as 'high-kings' over a multiplicity of lesser powers; and also a tradition of succession contests between different branches of the royal line. Practically every revolt in eleventh, twelfth and early thirteenth-century Scotland represented either regional particularism (Moray and early thirteenth century troubles in Caithness) or claims by members of the royal family (conflicts between Donald bàn and Donald II and ultimately Edgar; and the long line of northern revolts involving the descendants of William fitz Duncan, a son of Duncan II, revolts which extended through to the early thirteenth century). It is hard to see anti-English hostility as more than one element among many in these revolts.

The second problem which followed from the English connections of the Scottish royal family lay in the future, at the end of the thirteenth century, for these close connections and the encouragement which they gave to English notions of feudal superiority, were, under Edward I, to prove a source of centuries of conflict.

These English claims to superiority had a long history, going back to the grandiose titles adopted by the tenth century kings of Wessex; for example, *Æthelstanus basileos Anglorum et aeque tocius Brittaniae orbis gubernator* (Athelstan, Emperor of the English and likewise governor of the entire British world), *Eadmundus rex Anglorum caeterarumque gentium in circuitu persistentium gubernator et rector* (Edmund king of the English and governor and ruler of the other peoples surrounding them).[41] There was an uncertainty and lack of distinction between the realms of Scotland and England – particularly northern England, where the early kingdom of Strathclyde extended into Cumbria, and Bernicia and later Northumbria reached at times to the Forth. This vagueness was ultimately to extend to the nature of the authority which the later kings of Wessex and England, including Cnut, might claim. When kings of Scots were established, as Malcolm Canmore and Edgar were, by English intervention; and when Scottish kings or nobles, like Prince David in 1113, and Malcolm IV in 1159, joined in the campaigns of English kings in Wales and France, precedents were accumulating to support English claims of overlordship. In 1174, William the Lion joined in what proved to be a futile rising of English and Norman barons against Henry II, and after his defeat and capture at Alnwick, was forced, in the Treaty of Falaise (1174), to acknowledge Henry II's overlordship;[42] and Henry acted on this, holding castles in Scotland as a pledge for William's observance of the treaty, and intervening directly in succession conflicts in Galloway. The Treaty of Falaise was formally cancelled by the Quitclaim of Canterbury of 1189, when Henry's son, Richard I, in return for a payment of 10 000 merks, gave up all rights derived from the treaty of 1174; but this explicitly left unaffected all previous rights of the kings of England as they had existed in the reign of king Malcolm.[43] Cordial relations with the kings of England were normally good policy, and often stood the kings of Scots in good stead; but they could involve compromising precedents which could be made use of by Edward I in the years after the tragic death of Alexander III in 1286.

Till that disaster, however, the connections with England did not present a problem. Scotland remained a single kingdom, recognising a single king, who embodied in his person the identity which had come to encompass all its parts.

The solidarity of that kingdom was symbolised in the rituals at the time of the succession of the seven-year-old Alexander III in 1249. Then, if ever, one would have expected the identity of Scotland to shatter. There had been considerable baronial conflict in the 1240s when the Comyn and Dunbar factions had resorted to violence at the expense of the family of Bisset, whom the king had been unable to protect;[44] the unexpected death of Alexander II in 1249 might easily have led to open violence between Earl Walter Comyn and Alan Durward, the justiciar and leading adviser to the late king since about 1244; and, indeed, during the minority of Alexander III, there was much rivalry between the Comyn and Durward factions, which provoked Henry III to intervene to maintain the peace. Again, the striking thing is that the kingdom was unshaken. This owed something to Henry III's restraint: he was clearly anxious to do nothing to damage the standing of his daughter, who was Queen of Scots, following her marriage to the young Alexander III in 1251, and of her husband, the young king. It was also due to the evident

44

concern of the Scottish nobles to maintain the crown and kingdom. They tried, successfully, to counteract the effect of a minority by rituals which deliberately emphasised the unity and identity of the kingdom, and which brought out also the manysidedness of that kingdom. There was strong emphasis on the collective responsibility of the nobles. Alan Durward evidently tried to maintain the dominance which he had enjoyed at the end of Alexander II's reign by claiming the right to knight the young Alexander before the coronation, a claim which by thirteenth century precedents, implied a claim to some sort of regency. In England, during the minority of Henry III, William Marshal, who knighted the young Henry III in 1216, later emerged as *rector regis et regni* (governor of the king and the kingdom). Durward's action might easily have opened the way to factional quarrels, but Walter Comyn's counter-proposal that they should proceed at once to the enthronement without knighting the young king, seems to have convinced the clergy and magnates who were present.[45]

The actual ceremony, the first enthronement in Scotland of which we have more than the briefest details, emphasised Alexander's place in the long line of Scottish kings which stretched back, in legend, far beyond Malcolm III. He was consecrated as king by the bishop of St Andrews, whose predecessors in the late eleventh and early twelfth centuries had held the title of *episcopus Scotiae* (Bishop of Scotland). He was placed on the throne of stone which was claimed to be a symbol of ancient Scottish monarchy, the seat on which the kings of Scots were supposed to have been inaugurated from their first arrival in Scotland in the sixth century; and an elderly highlander (a *Scotus montanus* in the account of the fourteenth century chronicler, John of Fordun) recited his genealogy in Gaelic far back into the mists of the early Scottish kings.[46] These ceremonies were clearly perceived as important in proclaiming the identity of the Scottish kingdom, for they were described in detail in the fourteenth and fifteenth century chronicles of Fordun and Bower, who were, as we shall see in chapter 5, much obsessed with emphasising a national

45

identity against the English. Although these sources are late, the details they give are likely to be accurate. The ceremony of the recitation of ancestors would hardly have occurred to writers of the fourteenth and fifteenth centuries if it had not been part of genuine rituals; they would certainly not have attributed it to a highlander if they were not following a tradition, for by Fordun's time, the highlanders were regarded as 'wild Scots' in contrast to the more civilised lowlanders, and in some sense were already seen as outsiders in Scottish society. The lists of kings given in these accounts were not invented but derived from genuine ancient lists.[47]

Because this is much the fullest account of a medieval Scottish inauguration, it has been closely examined.[48] Much has been made of the peculiar features of the Scottish rite: the king was not crowned or anointed, as most kings in western Europe had been since the ninth or tenth centuries, but simply seated on a sacred throne of stone as a symbol of his choice and acceptance by the nobles. The recitation of his ancestry, as proof that he belonged to a royal kin, seems to derive, like the stone seat used in the ceremony, from ancient Ireland.

If we can believe Ailred of Rievaulx, David I found the Scottish rituals which he had to undergo deeply offensive.[49] Unfortunately. Ailred gives us no idea what it was that so offended the pious David: nothing in the ceremony of 1249 seems likely to cause such a reaction. So far from being an outrageous and primitive ceremony, enthronement was and is essential to any royal inauguration.[50] The lack of coronation and unction, the principal part of the religious ceremonies, was certainly regarded as a humiliating omission, which Alexander II had tried to remedy by appeals to Rome in 1221 and again in 1233. Unfortunately, these religious rites had been added to the secular enthronement ceremonies at a time when Scotland was isolated from the mainstream church by the Scandinavian settlements in northern England and Ireland; and by the time relations were re-established by St Margaret and her sons, formal authorisation by the papacy was regarded as necessary. This could be blocked by English pressure, as were both attempts by Alexander II when the English were anxious to maintain the inferior status of the Scottish kings by insisting that they had never before been crowned and should not be then. Yet Scottish kings are regularly depicted wearing a crown. The absence of the formal ceremonies of coronation and unction, which were first authorised for the coronation of David II in 1329, certainly did not mean that earlier Scottish inaugurations were purely secular occasions. Bishops are specifically mentioned as taking part in 1249; and in Alexander II's inauguration in 1214. It was the bishops who persuaded David I to undergo the 'horrible rites', whatever they may have been, in 1124. Perhaps some earlier and more primitive fertility ritual which had lapsed by 1249?

What does emerge is that the rites of 1249 were carefully planned to represent the unity of all the elements in the kingdom. The church was there in the persons of the Bishops of St Andrews and Dunkeld, who 'consecrated' the king (the same word is used in the accounts of earlier inaugurations); the nobility, in the person of the senior earl, the Earl of Fife, who enthroned the king; while the recitation of ancestors recalled that the kingdom of Scots could trace its origins to the even more ancient royal kin of the Dalriadic Scots in Ireland, a recognition of the extensive Gaelic-speaking areas subject to King Alexander. As we shall see, this claim of ancient origin was to become a fundamental point in the later assertions of an independent Scottish identity. The ceremonies of 1249 drew together all the threads which made up the thirteenth-century kingdom.

Six months later, in 1250, the coronation was followed by another highly significant ritual: the translation of the remains of St Margaret to a shrine in the abbey church of Dunfermline, in the presence of the young king, seven bishops and seven earls. This was the culmination of a campaign for her canonisation which had been going on since 1245.[51] Saints in the thirteenth century had important political overtones, witness the devotion of Henry III to St Edward the Confessor, which underlined Henry's place in a line of kings which went back before 1066; and the rebuilding of St Edward's church of Westminster as a more impressive royal abbey, the ritual centre of English monarchy. The later development of the cult of St Louis in France similarly emphasised the status of the Capetian dynasty. In Scotland, the cult of St Margaret emphasised both the Christianity and the identity of Scotland, under the dynasty of which she was, with her husband, the founder. It was significant that the translation of St Margaret could not proceed until the remains of her husband, Malcolm III, were also translated with her. The account was that her shrine was so heavy that it could not be moved, till Malcolm's grave was also opened; when both proved to be easily transportable! The emphasis was as much on Margaret's position in the dynasty as on her personal sanctity.

The thirteenth century, and particularly the reign of Alexander III, saw a significant extension of the area under the control of the king. Alexander II, after a reign which saw considerable efforts to emphasise his control over the remoter parts of his kingdom, had fallen ill and died in 1249 at Kerrera, in the Firth of Lorne, to the west of Oban, during an expedition designed to complete the subjugation of the hitherto Scandinavian Western Isles. Alexander III himself took up that task in his twenties, and after the battle of Largs in 1263, and Haakon Haakonson's subsequent death, was able in 1266 to secure the cession of all the Western Isles from Haakon's successor, Magnus VII, thus gaining formal authority over all of modern Scotland save the Northern Isles, which remained Norwegian for another two centuries. His reign had opened with two rituals which emphasised both his place in the long line of early Scottish kings and his membership of the dynasty which had ruled Scotland since the eleventh century. Later accounts of Alexander's reign were to emphasise the unity and peace which flowed from the long traditions which he embodied; it was to be seen as the golden age of a united and peaceful kingdom before the troubles of war and recurrent invasion descended on the land for over two centuries.[52]

This chapter has reviewed the political formation of that kingdom. Before we turn to the time of troubles which followed Alexander's death in 1286, we must look at the contribution of the church to the formation of a sense of Scottish identity; for, long before 1286, the Scottish church had been insisting on and defending its position as an independent unit in western Christendom, and in doing so, did much to develop the notion of Scotland as an independent identity.

3

THE IDENTITY OF FAITH

When in the ninth century the kingdoms of the Picts and Scots merged, there had already been a bond between them in the common Christian faith which both professed. Naturally, in a land of so many people, each one developed its own church, and there were differences of organisation and traditions between them. But England too in the age of the conversion was a land of many peoples; and yet Bede, writing in the eighth century and treating of the history of at least eight 'kingdoms', could still write an 'Ecclesiastical History of the English People'. For him they were one people in Christ and had one history. So for the Scots, Christianity was to be a unifier, a loyalty that joined Picts and Scots, Celt and Saxon, Briton and in the end Scandinavian, though the last was the most difficult.

The Christian church in Scotland, however, as it developed from around the fifth century AD, was formed into a number of 'parishes', each bound together by an allegiance to a particular missionary saint and marked out by church dedications to his or her name, though the 'parish' had developed through the work of unrecorded missionary followers over many generations.[1] There was a church of St Ninian, centred at Whithorn, extending from the south-west well into central Scotland, and even Fife. From there, St Kentigern, in the sixth century, seems to have created a new

50

'parish' centred perhaps on Govan or Inchinnan, south of the Clyde, rather than at the present site of Glasgow Cathedral, which has produced no early relics. His was to be a church of Strathclyde, much more specifically than Ninian's. St Columba, who came to the Scots of Dalriada in Argyll as an exile from Ireland in the sixth century, established the church of Iona, from which there were founded many later monasteries – his was a specifically monastic church: these early 'parishes' had very varied organisation. In the sixth and seventh centuries, the Columban church was restricted to western Argyll and the isles around Mull, the land of the Scots of Dalriada. Later other 'parishes' developed in the Hebrides – taking as their special dedicatees St Donan and St Maelrubai. Meanwhile, St Aidan, who went from Iona in the seventh century to Lindisfarne on the Northumbrian coast, set up a church which expanded from Northumbria in the seventh and eighth centuries to establish an offshoot in south-east Scotland, which was developed by St Baldred at North Berwick, and extended at times into Fife. By the end of the seventh century what was to be Scotland had a complex, informally organised and sometimes overlapping collection of Christian churches; roughly corresponding to the various peoples who then occupied the land.

But the religion that began by crossing the barriers between Jew and Gentile crossed ethnic barriers in Scotland and elsewhere with astounding ease, given the difficulties of communication at the time, both geographical and linguistic. St Ninian was venerated far outside the limits of Galloway; St Patrick went from Britons to Irish, the Irish and the English were missionaries to the German tribes beyond the Rhine, St Columba himself travelled to the Picts, though his 'mission' may have been less an effort to convert Bridei, king of the Picts, than a piece of diplomacy, trying to secure his protection for Christian monks who wanted to settle in Orkney.[2] The effective conversion of the Picts probably came in the eighth century and from Northumbria.[3] In Northumbria itself, there were missions and influences in the early seventh century successively from Canterbury (converted directly from Rome by St Augustine from 597) to Edwin's kingdom of Deira, around York in the 620s; and from Iona, in the 630s and later to the more northern kingdom of Bernicia, on the coast of the later Northumberland. So Northumbrian Christianity as it developed was itself a blend of Irish and 'Roman' influences. Christianity was not the property of any single culture or society; both in England and Scotland it could be a powerful bond between diverse peoples.

The development of the church was inevitably affected by secular politics. Scotland was a far more diverse society than Anglo-Saxon England; and there were no equivalents to the 'Bretwaldas' who acted as intermittent high kings and whose careers provide the focus for Bede's 'History' which transcends individual kingdoms. Dark Age Scotland had no Bede, and no single 'history' to impose a sense of higher unity. For Scotland, paradoxically, it was the descent of the Vikings in the eighth and ninth centuries which acted as the catalyst for union, both between secular powers and between ecclesiastical 'parishes'. Shetland, Orkney, Caithness, Sutherland and the Western Isles became part of an aggressive Scandinavian world, itself divided among chieftains subject to little control from Norway or anywhere else, and all ready to attack wherever they found wealth and plunder.

Before the Viking raids, Iona had become the greatest shrine in Scotland, largely due to the efforts of Adomnan, abbot from 679 to 704. His 'Life of St Columba',[4] written around 690, with its emphasis on Columba's personal piety and sanctity and on the miracles he worked, was in a sense a defence of the Columban church against what might seem the imperialism of the Northumbrian church and kingdom. The Northumbrian church had briefly established a bishopric at Abercorn on the Forth, and Egfrith, King of Northumbria, had tried to extend his authority into Pictland.[5] Adomnan's account of Columba, written after the collapse of this Northumbrian attempt in 685 at the Battle of Nechtansmere, in Angus, effectively raised Columba from the apostle of a part of Dalriada into the apostle of the Scots as a whole.

The descent of the Vikings put all this into question. They made a particular target of religious houses, probably not so much because they were hostile to the church as because they knew treasures would be found there. Iona was sacked in 795 and again in 802. In 806 the 68 monks of the community were 'slain by the gentiles' (i.e. Vikings). Iona was becoming uninhabitable. In 807 the abbot withdrew to Kells in Ireland with the relics of St Columba. Yet for the Scots on both sides of the Irish Sea, Iona was still the centre of their faith; and for a time, whenever possible despite all the dangers, abbots returned to there with their relics and monks remained, sometimes to be martyred.[6]

In 849, the then abbot of Iona is said, in the Annals of Ulster, to have moved the relics of Columba yet again to Ireland; while Kenneth mac Alpin, according to the earliest version of the Chronicles of the Kings of Scots, removed the relics in the same year to a church he had built, by which is almost certainly meant Dunkeld.[7] This may suggest that the relics were shared between the two. The abbot of Kenneth's new monastery at Dunkeld seems to have become the bishop of the new united kingdom of Picts and Scots, with its centre in the Tay valley and its chief church at Dunkeld. In 865, according to the Annals of Ulster, there died 'Tuathal, chief bishop of Fortriu' (i.e. the area centering on the Tay valley) 'and abbot of Dunkeld'.[8]

The Picts, however, had their own contribution to make to this Christian kingdom, for they, like the Scots, had been Christian for some time. We have little firm information on how they were converted, but Nechtan, King of the Picts from 706, despite the earlier attack by King Egfrith was nevertheless anxious in the end to establish links with the Christian church in Northumbria, which had itself been going through many changes in the previous half-century. Since the work of St Wilfrid, whose long career spanned the period from the 660s till his death in 709, and of Benedict Biscop, the founder of the Abbeys of Wearmouth and Jarrow, the Northumbrian church had been much more closely linked to Rome and the Mediterranean traditions, which formed the mainstream of the church. Nechtan was clearly concerned to be in touch with those traditions. Some time before 714, he wrote to Coelfrith, Abbot of Wearmouth in Northumbria, seeking not only a formal refutation of Irish errors over Easter, which had been a major issue in the conflict between the 'Celtic' and 'Roman' traditions for almost a century, but much more significantly, for architects 'to make a church of stone among his people after the manner of the Romans'.[9] Pictland, in the early eighth century, was forging links with the Northumbrian province of the church. At Rosemarkie in Ross and Cromarty there was already in the early eighth century a church dedicated to St Peter and a Bishop Curitan who seems to have taken the Latin name of Boniface. Since there were other dedications to St Peter in the Pictish area, Professor Duncan has suggested the existence of a 'Romanising group among Nechtan's clergy' who 'may have been led by Curitan'.[10] Most significantly of all for the future, there was, by the middle of the eighth century, an abbot at Kilrymond in Fife, whose church was probably dedicated to St Andrew, for St Andrews became the name of the settlement that grew up round it.[11] By the same period, Pictish symbol stones, a type of monument previously entirely pagan, begin to show Christian symbolism.

The union of Picts and Scots in the ninth century thus brought together two distinct Christian traditions: the Columban, by now formally brought into line with the main stream of the church, since Iona accepted 'Roman' practices in the early eighth century, and represented, after 849, by the relics of St Columba at Dunkeld; and the Pictish, with its Northumbrian links, and now a Biblical patron in St Andrew.

It remains a paradox that the religious centre of the Scottish kingdom was neither Iona, which allegedly retained for long its symbolic significance as the burial place of Scottish kings (the last to be so buried was Donald bàn who was deposed in 1097), nor Dunkeld in the heart of Scotland, not far from what became the normal site of royal inaugurations at Scone; but in a small east-coast settlement where the town that grew up did not play any important part in the government of Scotland. Nor, though it possessed a harbour, was it ever to be a particularly prominent port. St Andrews seems to have owed its position entirely to the cult of St Andrew. How this came about remains very obscure. Later accounts emphasise the early arrival of relics of St Andrew, brought by St Rule (Regulus) to Scotland in the mid-4th century.[12] This unlikely tale is only recorded in versions of the legend produced in or after the twelfth century, though elements in it may well be older. The story looks, in the form in which we have it, like propaganda for St Andrews as the sacred heart of the more recently unified kingdom.

By whatever means St Andrews became the seat of the 'Bishop of Alba', the real point is that the Christian church had become closely linked with the idea of a kingdom of the Scots; and that the Scottish church had acquired a focus. Devotion to St Columba, and then to St Andrew, had become an expression of a wider unity. The Christian church was to be a bond tying together the various peoples who inhabited the land; it gave an authority to the kings who ruled the land under God, an authority of which they were conscious and did everything they could to exploit. Hence, the identity of faith became an important element in the identity of Scotland.

Yet the place of the faith in a Scottish identity was to be at times ambiguous. For two centuries or so after the union of Picts and Scots in the ninth century, the period during which St Andrews emerged as the dominant ecclesiastical centre of the kingdom, Scotland and its church were in a sense cut off from the mainstream of Christendom by the ninth century Scandinavian settlements in the north of England and Ireland, which meant a barrier between the Scots and the increasingly politically and culturally dominant power of Wessex. Though the Scandinavian kingdom of York collapsed in 954, the church in Northumbria hardly revived till the recovery under the Normans in the late eleventh century. We know very little in detail of what was happening in Scotland, but its church appears to have been isolated and left behind at a time when the tenth-century monastic reforms on the Continent associated with Cluny and Gorze were transforming the church at large, restoring the influence of the Benedictine rule, emphasising the freedom of the church from lay control and its devotion to the papacy, and attracting the support of the nobility for new monastic foundations.

The Scandinavian barrier, however, was not permanent. The rulers of York and Dublin, strong though they might be militarily, proved far less stable than the kings of Wessex and of the Picts and Scots; and it was perhaps inevitable that their power, at least in the north of England, should crumble. Gradually, the authority of Wessex penetrated the north and by the tenth century the issue was where would lie the limits of English and Scottish power. Behind the screen of the Danish conquests, the kings of Scots had been extending their authority over both Lothian and Strathclyde; and as, in the tenth century, the Danish kingdoms lost their independence, the Scots came into direct contact with the rulers of Wessex, albeit at the limits of their still hardly consolidated power. By this time Strathclyde had become, to adapt the words of Professor Smyth, a 'satellite'[13] of the kings of Scots; and Lothian seems to have been recognised formally as subject to Kenneth II, king of Scots from 971 to 995, as part of a settlement with King Edgar of Wessex around 973. The position was consolidated by the victory in 1016 or 1018 of Malcolm II, King of Scots from 1005 to 1034, over the Northumbrian Earl Uhtred at Carham, just on what is now the English side of the Tweed between Coldstream and Kelso.

In this situation, any attempt to 'modernise' the Scottish church might easily have opened it to influences from England, influences which might make it less a focus for a distinct Scottish identity. In the event this did not happen: the church became one of the foremost upholders of a Scottish identity. But in the late eleventh century the possibility of its losing its Scottish focus was real.

This became explicit in the policies of William the Conqueror after 1069 when he had consolidated his grip on England. For many, England might have seemed enough to cope with; and indeed what Professor Douglas has called the 'conjoint realm' of England and Normandy did indeed prove quite enough for William to handle. But in the early 1070s, he clearly had some conception of reviving the claims of tenth-century kings to overriding authority over all the British Isles and, as we have seen, invaded Scotland in 1072 and was able to compel Malcolm III to pay him homage.

This clear threat to Scottish independence extended explicitly to the Scottish church. At Easter 1072, before William's expedition to Scotland, an agreement was reached in his presence in a dispute caused by the determination of Lanfranc, Archbishop of Canterbury, to secure a submission from the new Archbishop of York, Thomas of Bayeux. In this settlement, Lanfranc was recognised as *primas totius Britannie* (primate of all Britain); under him, there was conceded to the Archbishop of York the submission of the Bishop of Durham and 'of all regions from the limits of the bishopric of Lichfield and the Humber to the ultimate limits of Scotland'.[14] In William's eyes, there was to be one church for the entire British Isles, and its overall primate was to be the Archbishop of Canterbury; and for Scotland and the north of England immediately, the archbishop was to be York. This scheme followed the prescription of Gregory I in one of his letters to St Augustine.[15] Its revival, with at least the implication that it represented practical politics, was a clear declaration of English intentions which were to apply to both church and state.

The circumstances of the Scottish church in the late eleventh century made the danger even more pressing. The monastic reforms of Cluny, Fleury and Gorze on the Continent, of Dunstan, Oswald and Æthelwold in England, had had no effect on monasteries in Northumbria or further

57

north: the church in Scotland remained a mixture of communities based on early Celtic monasticism, of ill-defined groups of clergy reminiscent of Anglo-Saxon minsters (the 'culdees' or *céle De*, vassals of God), with some rather vague semblance of an episcopal organisation – several bishops are mentioned but it is hard to see exactly the organisation they represented. Yet the reigns of Malcolm III (1057–93) and William the Conqueror (1066–87) coincided with the full impact of the Gregorian reforms, which, under the leadership of Gregory VII, Pope from 1073 to 1085, aimed to end lay domination of the church and, under the papacy, remove abuses and establish the authority of canon law. If the Scottish church was to be brought into line, it was surely from England that the reforms had immediately to come.

The credit for initiating reform has always been given to the English princess, Margaret, the second wife of Malcolm Canmore from around 1070 till they both died within days of each other in 1093. Despite her enormous reputation, we know very little that is definite about her. A granddaughter of Edmund Ironside, King of England briefly in 1016, and daughter of Agatha, a relative of the Emperor Henry II, she was very well connected but brought up in exile in the recently converted kingdom of Hungary. Her aunt by marriage was the daughter of St Stephen, the King of Hungary who is credited with the conversion of his kingdom in AD 1000, so Margaret probably received a strongly Christian upbringing. With her brother, Edgar Ætheling, she took refuge in Scotland in 1067 and soon after (perhaps in 1070) she married King Malcolm, reluctantly according to the Worcester version of the Anglo-Saxon Chronicle, for she would have preferred a life of religion.[16] (What happened to Malcolm's first wife Ingibiorg is unknown.) The Anglo-Saxon Chronicle summarises almost all that we really know of Margaret, and its account is vague indeed. 'She was destined to increase the glory of God in that land, to turn the king aside from the path of error, to incline him together with his people towards a better way of life, and to abolish the vices which that nation had indulged in in the past – all of which she subsequently accomplished.'[17] There is a biography, almost certainly written by Turgot, Prior of Durham, confidant of Queen Margaret, and later Bishop of St Andrews, but it is little more than a lengthy and unspecific embroidery on these themes.[18] Margaret's descendants occupied the throne from 1097 to 1286, and she became something of a patron saint to the line, canonised and her remains translated with elaborate ceremony in 1250 to a shrine in the church she had apparently founded at Dunfermline. It is, however, very hard to penetrate to the facts behind the hagiography.

What is clear is that her efforts to 'reform' the Scottish church had perforce to rely on help from England and, indeed, brought out all the dangers of that process. We know that she turned to Lanfranc, for a letter from him in response to her approach survives. He sends her three monks from Canterbury to help in her work and asks her to 'endeavour resolutely and effectively to complete what you have begun for God and for your souls'.[19] Most of his letter, however, is an expression of his delight, mingled with humility, that she should have chosen him as her spiritual father. Was this delight not perhaps connected with the idea that this went some way towards recognising his position as *primas totius Britannie*?

England, with its many reformed houses, was the obvious place to turn for help in reforming and modernising the Scottish church: Scottish houses, founded at Dunfermline by Margaret herself and at Scone by her son Alexander I, were started by colonies of monks and canons from England. The future David I did indeed look to Thiron in France for monks for a monastery at Selkirk, founded around 1113, later moved to Kelso. That, however, remained an isolated example. Most Scottish monasteries in the twelfth century were founded from English houses, and were part of monastic orders which were the 'multi-national corporations' of the twelfth century. Cistercians in particular, one of the new orders founded at the end of the eleventh century, took a wide view of their connections. Melrose, one of the leading Scottish Cistercian houses, produced in the twelfth and thirteenth centuries a chronicle which is one of the main Scottish narrative sources of the period.[20] To read it is to experience a view of the times which is far more centred on the Cistercian order in Britain than on the history of Scotland. Events are described, briefly and usually accurately. But the chroniclers are far more interested in Cistercian personalia than in Scottish history. The text is full of mentions of moves, when for instance an Abbot of Melrose becomes Abbot of Rievaulx, of which Melrose was a daughter house, or monks of Melrose become abbots of Coupar Angus, in its turn a daughter of Melrose, or bishops of Moray or of Down in Ireland. The Cistercians were a particularly close-knit body: abbeys were founded by the dispatch of a core of monks from a 'mother-house' and the mother-house remained to a degree in authority over her daughters, appointing their abbot and 'visiting' them to check that all was well. Hence the career-patterns already mentioned, and the particularly close sense of belonging to a network which transcended local bounds of authority within the secular world.

Important also for the future of the church in Scotland was the tightening of authority within the church at large, which was the main result of the Gregorian reform movement. This movement is often seen as an attempt by the church to establish authority over lay rulers. Such it was in part. Henry II in England indeed failed ultimately to resist papal authority in the Becket controversy; King John likewise failed in the end over the appointment of Stephen Langton as Archbishop of Canterbury. On the other hand, William the Lion of Scotland was more successful in getting his candidate eventually elected to St Andrews in 1189 in a less celebrated but equally significant quarrel which had lasted since 1178. Whatever victories the popes of the twelfth century may have achieved in some of these striking conflicts, they certainly had to leave kings a large measure of authority in practice over their churches, over appointments to sees and abbacies in particular.

But over the church, especially in matters of canon law, the authority of the papacy was secured by the Gregorian reforms. With considerable prescience, the German bishops who supported the Emperor Henry IV against Gregory VII in 1076 claimed that Gregory wished to subvert the traditional authority of the ordinary (i.e. the diocesan bishop).[21] They were right, and he did. By the mid-twelfth century, Archbishop Theobald of Canterbury was to find that he could hardly maintain the authority of his court because whenever he was on the point of pronouncing judgment against anyone within his jurisdiction, the errant, be he cleric or lay, simply appealed to the Pope, which at once took the case out of his power![22] Papal jurisdiction came to operate as extensively in Scotland as anywhere else; and hence Scotland became subject to an authority which saw itself as being, at least in theory, beyond local and secular divisions. The papacy was a universal authority and determined to act as such.

This obviously created a tension between the sense of the church as embodying a Scottish unity and the sense of it as part of a universal Christian order. In general throughout Christendom this tension was not extreme, coming to the surface only in celebrated cases of conflict. Normally the papacy and the religious orders, though conscious of their universal status, were careful to balance this by a recognition of local identities. Authority was presumed but local susceptibilities treated with care.

Scotland, however, had a special problem. During Malcolm III's reign, there was from around 1070 a 'Bishop of Alba', Fothad, based at St Andrews. It is not clear what authority this bishop had over any others that may have existed – the whole situation is unclear. Scotland does not appear to have had any settled provincial organisation. And when Alexander I, at the beginning of his reign in 1107, some considerable time after Fothad's death in 1093, sought a new bishop, he turned to Turgot, Prior of Durham and almost certainly the author of the biography of Queen Margaret. After Turgot's death in 1115, Alexander looked again to England, this time to

Canterbury and to Eadmer, the biographer of St Anselm. Distinguished as both authors, especially Eadmer, were, neither seems to have been a success as bishop; indeed Eadmer, for reasons to which we shall return, never got as far as consecration. And thereafter, Alexander turned to Robert Prior of Scone, though even he came originally from Nostell near Pontefract in Yorkshire.

There was at the beginning of the twelfth century a very real danger that Scotland might be absorbed ecclesiastically into England, and become a part of the province of York, as had been envisaged in the settlement of 1072 between Lanfranc and Thomas of York. Successive archbishops of York were very well aware of this and were to press their claims whenever possible. Tidy minds at Rome might see the logic of this: Gregory I's notion of a church of Britain was appealing, and Rome probably had little grasp of the political complexity of these remote islands. Yet in the end this did not happen. Kings and churchmen maintained their identity and their independence.

How did this come about? In part it was the doing of the kings. Malcolm Canmore performed homage to William in 1072; but whatever obligations he may have conceived himself as undertaking evidently sat very lightly upon him, since he subsequently invaded England three more times, in 1079, 1091 and finally in the expedition on which he was killed in 1093. He was also perhaps aware of the danger of ecclesiastical imperialism. In 1074, two members of the community of Durham tried to set up a cell or hermitage on the now desolate site of St Cuthbert's early monastery at Melrose. Malcolm seems not to have objected in principle to a new religious establishment, but he was determined that they should recognise that it was being set up in Scotland and they should therefore perform fealty to him. Why they refused is not clear; but they were ordered to withdraw by the Bishop of Durham, Walcher, who was probably anxious, in an exposed position, not unnecessarily to incur the hostility of the king of Scots.[23] There seems to have been no personal animosity; for one of the two was Turgot, subsequently Prior of Durham and eventually Bishop of St Andrews.

Later kings, as we have seen, had an ambivalent relationship with England. Edgar had been placed on the throne in 1097 as a protégé of William Rufus; David I was brought up at Henry's court, served Henry in his wars and led the Scots at the battle of the Standard in 1138 in support of the claims of Henry's daughter Matilda. Malcolm IV joined in Henry II's Toulouse campaign in 1159 and accepted knighthood from him at Tours. At least one Scottish king, however, Alexander I (1107–24), of whom little else is known, was clearly determined to uphold the independence of his church against the claims of both York and Canterbury. He chose Turgot, Prior of Durham, as his bishop for the long vacant see of St Andrews, a nomination for which he needed and obtained the consent of Henry I, since Turgot was in the latter's allegiance. Nevertheless, Alexander, and we are told the church of St Andrews, refused to contemplate any profession to York, and on this ground, and because of a vacancy at York, Turgot's consecration was delayed for something like two years. In the end it was Henry I who resolved the matter by requiring the new Archbishop of York to consecrate Turgot without demanding an immediate profession, though reserving the positions of York and St Andrews for future settlement. Henry clearly upheld William the Conqueror's position of 1072 that the Scottish church was part of his responsibilities, but Alexander had avoided any formal submission to York.[24]

This remained Alexander's tactics. When he turned to Eadmer as his choice for his second Bishop of St Andrews, it was probably with the idea that a monk of Canterbury was least of all likely to acquiesce in the claims of York. In this he was perfectly correct. On being offered the position, one of Eadmer's first acts was to get a very cogently argued brief from Nicholas, Prior of Worcester, clearly an expert canonist and legal tactician, on the alleged fallacies in the York claim and how to counter it in practical tactics.[25] Eadmer, however, as a monk of Canterbury, was devoted to the rights of that see, and tried to insist on making his profession to its archbishop, Ralph. Alexander would have none of it: he claimed in a letter to the Archbishop of Canterbury that Eadmer refused to accept the customs of Scotland and rather than do so, wished to be released from his position. As Archbishop Ralph pointed out, in a letter acknowledging Eadmer's return to Canterbury, this was not exactly Eadmer's account of the quarrel, which we can find in his *Historia Novorum*.[26] The conclusion was that Alexander did not permit the profession to Canterbury and Eadmer withdrew.

Generally, however, the Scottish church seems to have been left to fight its own battle for independence – and it proved to be a hard and long fight. The papacy was, for more than half a century, a consistent supporter of the claims of York to supremacy over the Scottish church; and the position of the Scots, throughout that period, was weakened by an apparent tendency in Rome, and perhaps in Scotland itself, to see what we now think of as the 'Scottish' church in two parts: *Scotia*, Scotland north of the Forth, and the church of Cumbria or Strathclyde which meant the sees of Glasgow and perhaps Whithorn. Not till a bull of Adrian IV in 1155 is the Bishop of Glasgow listed along with the rest of the Scottish bishops, not till a still later bull of the same pope, issued between 1157 and 1159, do we have the address to 'Bishop Robert of St Andrews, the bishop of Glasgow and the rest of the bishops of Scotland'.[27] All were in any case seen as subject to York.

Demands for obedience to York are the recurrent theme of papal bulls to the Scottish bishops for the first half of the twelfth century. The first bull addressed to the Scottish bishops of which we have the text, issued by Paschal II at the turn of the years 1100 and 1101, was a command to them to show obedience to the newly appointed Archbishop Gerard of York. The command was later repeated by Calixtus II (1119–24), Honorius II (1124–30), Innocent II (1130–43), Eugenius III (1145–53), Anastasius IV (1153–4), Adrian IV (1154–9) and, finally, by Alexander III in 1162. It is obvious from the constant repetition of this command – several of these popes issued it more than once – that the Scottish bishops were holding very consistently to their refusal. The bulls were probably all issued at the request of frustrated archbishops of York, who could do very little else to try to enforce their authority. It is hard to know how far the popes were really concerned to do anything. Once, in 1125, Honorius II sent a legate to investigate:[28] we know little of what he did; but Honorius continued formally to support the claims of York, as did Adrian IV, despite, probably also formally, offering the Scots a chance to put forward any case they had against the claims. Something has been made of this last offer, but it seems in fact little more than the command 'Do this or show that you should not', a cautious formula, leaving open the possibility of legal argument.[29] It is more than most of Adrian's predecessors offered. At the same time, the popes were willing to continue issuing, probably equally formally, protections and privileges for Scottish sees and monasteries.

The continued defiance of the Scots was in fact a serious blow to York's claims, for it was just at this point, in the first half of the twelfth century, that Scotland was acquiring a diocesan episcopate. Under Malcolm III (1057–93), there were references to Fothad, as 'chief bishop of Alba', who died in 1093.[30] His successor Turgot is described in a friendly letter from Pope Paschal II, written between 1112 and 1114 as '*Scottorum episcopus*', Bishop of the Scots.[31] By the time of Adrian IV in 1155, there were bishops of Aberdeen, Brechin, Caithness, Dunblane, Dunkeld, Glasgow, Moray, Ross and Whithorn as well as St Andrews.[32] A formidable body of suffragans was resisting subordination to York. Yet there was no clear sign of a provincial organisation and no formal head to this church. In practice, St Andrews was treated as senior; but the position of Glasgow and Whithorn was still ill-defined. Were they included among the bishoprics of the Scots, or were Cumbria and Strathclyde still regarded as separate? Much had still to be clarified about the structures of the Scottish church, beyond the question of submission to York.

The catalyst seems to have come, somewhat surprisingly, in an English issue unconnected with Scotland: the Becket controversy. The Pope, Alexander III, who succeeded Adrian IV in 1159, was weakened by the challenge of an anti-pope, supported by the Emperor Frederick Barbarossa. He was therefore anxious to do anything possible to win or retain the backing of Henry II, who might otherwise easily be persuaded to support the imperial anti-pope. Close to Henry II by this time was Roger of Pont l'Evêque, Archbishop of York. Certainly, Alexander had at this point some interest in not alienating either unnecessarily. Hence no doubt the bull of September 1162,[33] repeating Adrian IV's bull of 1155 ordering the Scottish bishops to obey the Archbishop of York as their metropolitan, or face papal censures, a bull which, as we shall see, took a line he was only to repeat in one other bull of uncertain date, which may be as early as May 1164, though other dates up to 1174 are possible.[34] Even in the early years of his troubled pontificate, it is uncertain how far Alexander was concerned to push the point: he issued at least seven papal privileges to Scottish abbeys and bishops between November 1162 and July 1164,[35] although the Scots were clearly not prepared to submit to York. Interesting evidence of this unwillingness emerged at the Council of Tours, which Alexander called in 1163, in somewhat improvised conditions, when he was in exile from Rome. We know the order of seating at the council, for it was recorded: metropolitans were normally accompanied by their sufragans. Canterbury and York were seated separately: *de provincia Cantuariensi* Becket with eleven suffragans; *de provincia Eboracensi* Roger with one only, Durham. The only Scot present, the Bishop of Dunkeld, appeared afar off: between Spain and the bishops of the Curia, who come at the end of the list and probably in the position of highest honour, there is *de Scotia, Dunkeldensis episcopus venit* – 'from Scotland there came the bishop of Dunkeld'![36] The Scots were holding firmly to their position as an independent entity.

Alexander, though an astute and careful politician, was much more than that. It is clear that the Becket controversy, when it really broke out in 1164, caused him grave political problems. He could certainly have done without it and, over the years, he did his best to restrain Becket. He clearly hoped for peace; but he also saw that the case involved principles on which he could not compromise. The Scots were to owe much to that clarity of vision.

In November 1164, there is a dramatic change in the papal attitude. Alexander could not yet have known in detail of the final rupture between Becket and Henry at Northampton. We do not know how much he knew of Roger of Pont l'Evêque's hostility to Becket. Alexander had, however, to deal with a request from Malcolm IV and the church of Glasgow that he consecrate, as bishop of that see, Ingram, Archdeacon of Glasgow and chancellor of the kingdom. All previous papal bulls on the matter of consecrations had stressed that Scottish bishops must be consecrated by the archbishops of York or otherwise with their permission. Alexander's bull, addressed to the Dean and Canons of Glasgow on 1 November 1164, reverses this: 'Although the emissaries of our venerable brother the archbishop of York ... who were present pressed us not to proceed, nevertheless we ... with the advice of our brethren [the cardinals] ... have consecrated him bishop. We therefore ... send him with the fullness of the grace and benediction of the apostolic see to you as our special sons and commend him to you.'[37] For the first time, the Pope has rejected the claims of York; and, more, he describes the canons of Glasgow as *speciales filios* of the Holy See, a technical term which, in a later bull to the Scots, was explained as implying direct subjection to the Holy See without any intermediary. It was an explicit rejection of the claims of York, by a Pope who fully understood the implications of what he was doing. That rejection seems to have been very quickly repeated when early in 1165 Roger of York failed to prevent the consecration of the elect of St Andrews by other Scottish bishops with papal authority.[38] These decisions confirmed half a century of insistence by the Scottish bishops and their kings that the Scottish church was an independent entity, subject neither to York nor Canterbury.

This was not the end of the matter; under William the Lion, king from 1165 to 1214, the Scottish church faced an even more dangerous antagonist, Henry II himself. When William was captured at Alnwick in 1174, this gave Henry the chance to assert his dominance. William, by the treaty of Falaise of that year, was forced to concede control of several Scottish castles and accept a formal subordination to Henry, including a recognition that 'the church of Scotland shall henceforward owe such subjection to the church of England as it should do, and was accustomed to do in the time of his predecessors as kings of England'. The bishops of Scotland are to accept this and swear fealty to Henry.[39] This treaty firmly contradicted Pope Alexander III's line which he had followed since 1164. In 1174, he had authorised the consecration of the elect of Glasgow, without any reference to the claims of York.[40] In the first few months of 1175, he issued a special protection for the church of Glasgow as the *specialem filiam nostram nullo mediante* ('our special daughter with no intermediary').[41] In 1176, he responded directly to the Treaty of Falaise. Henry II's action was 'an affront to God and to the pope himself, and an attack on ecclesiastical liberty. Kings and princes have no right to arrange ecclesiastical matters.' The liberty of the Scottish bishops was not to be diminished; the Archbishop of York was not to exercise metropolitan authority over them unless the Pope or his successors might find that this right was justified. Until and unless that might happen the bishops of Scotland are to show obedience to no-one except the Pope.[42] This seems an explicit cancellation, presumably at the request of the Scottish bishops, of the obligations undertaken under the treaty of Falaise.

Papal bulls did not necessarily settle the matter; but Henry II had much more on his mind than the subjugation of Scotland; and his successor had no wish to persist with either

Henry's political or ecclesiastical imperialism. As we saw in chapter 2, the Quitclaim of Canterbury of 1189 undid all the political concessions made by William the Lion in 1174. It made no reference to the church – presumably the English claims were recognised as overturned by Alexander's ruling of 1176; but perhaps to make sure, Celestine III issued in 1192 his famous bull *Cum Universi*, declaring that the Scottish church was the 'special daughter' of the papacy and subject directly to the Pope with no intermediary.[43] This made the essential point that the Scottish church was subject neither to York nor Canterbury. The bull was the culmination of almost a century of struggle by the Scots to maintain the separate identity of their church, at a time when no-one else was led to proclaim explicitly and repeatedly a distinctive Scottish identity. York clearly did not give up all hope – in the fifteenth century archbishops of York were still preserving copies of the papal bulls of the early twelfth century which proclaimed the supremacy of York over the Scottish church, and from their texts the copies came to be entered on a royal signet register, MS Harley 433, mainly known to historians as a record of the government of Richard III of England![44] But this was antiquarianism. The issue had been effectively settled in 1192.

There were, however, still problems over the organisation of the Scottish church. It was independent and subject only to Rome; but it had no agreed provincial head, or provincial organisation. By a bull of 1225, a provincial council of the Scottish church was established, to be presided over by a 'conservator' of the council, who was to be chosen for each occasion – there was not to be an archbishop in Scotland till 1472, when St Andrews was made an archbishopric, to be followed by Glasgow in 1492 – and this council was to act as the guiding authority of what was now clearly an independent church. Something of the kind was essential, for following the third Lateran Council in 1215 the church at large was entering a period of reform in which provinces and bishops were required to hold councils and enforce the decrees embodying Innocent III's great schemes of reform. This clearly was what brought the Scottish church councils into existence. From then on they were to meet frequently, though few formal records of their proceedings survive until the years immediately before the Reformation.[45]

By the early thirteenth century, therefore, the Scottish church had established a distinctive identity for itself and had at length persuaded the authorities of the church to recognise this identity.

This recognition naturally confirmed the role of churchmen in Scottish government; as chancellors and officials they had long taken their place beside the lay nobility in the king's counsels. Their position was already emphasised in the royal inaugurations where, as we have seen, Scottish kings were 'consecrated' by the church. Bishops are specifically mentioned as taking part in the inaugurations of William the Lion, Alexander II and Alexander III.[46] When it came to the crisis of 1286, the bishops of St Andrews and Glasgow joined two earls and two barons as 'Guardians' of the kingdom during the minority of the infant Queen Margaret, and after her death in the interregnum which followed.

This close linking of what we would now term 'church' and 'state' in upholding the national identity in this supreme crisis, was graphically expressed in the seal adopted by the Guardians. The obverse showed the royal arms of Scotland, the Lion Rampant within the double tressure flory counter-flory, with the legend SIGILLUM SCOCIE DEPUTATUM REGIMINI REGNI (the seal of Scotland appointed for the government of the kingdom); the reverse had St Andrew on his cross, with the legend ANDREA SCOTIS DUX ESTO COMPATRIOTIS (Andrew be leader of the compatriot Scots).[47] This is the first appearance of St Andrew as the 'patron saint' of Scotland; and his adoption in that role at the point when the Scottish identity was to face its most serious challenge, aptly emphasises the part of the church in creating and then in defending that identity.

4

THE WARS OF INDEPENDENCE

The challenge came when, on a stormy night in March 1286, Alexander III fell to his death at Kinghorn in Fife. He left no effective successor. His heir, duly accepted as Queen, was his granddaughter Margaret, aged at most four at the time and living at the court of her father Eric, King of Norway, whom Alexander's daughter, also called Margaret, had married in 1281. This latter Margaret had died in 1283. For Edward I, King of England and conqueror of Wales, Alexander's death presented an opportunity; though not one that he was in a particular hurry to take up.

Edward himself had business in France and Gascony and in a parliament which met on 23 April 1286 he announced his intention of going abroad to act as arbitrator in the long-running dispute between Charles of Anjou and Peter of Aragon over their rival claims to the kingdom of Sicily. This, for him, not very immediate issue seemed more pressing than any events in Scotland. The arbitration and other business in France and Gascony kept him abroad till 1289. Nevertheless, he was aware that there was now a chance to resolve the relationship between Scotland and England which had been an issue for every king of England at least since Henry II, but which had been comparatively dormant under his father and so far in his own reign. In 1278 Alexander III had skilfully sidestepped Edward's request for homage for the kingdom of

71

Scotland.[1] Edward was bound to see a royal minority as a chance to renew his claims; and as the sovereign was this time a girl, there opened the opportunity for an even more advantageous match for England. Edward may not have been in a hurry, but on his return in 1289, he pursued the project of a marriage between the six-or seven-year-old queen and his own five-year-old son, a marriage which was finally agreed by the treaty of Birgham in 1290.[2]

Edward's attitude towards Scotland was carefully thought out. He believed himself to be its overlord, and he certainly had the precedents of his father's actions in the 1250s, actions which the Scots at the time had seemed to accept. Yet it was obvious that Edward's intentions went beyond the helpful oversight that had apparently been welcome in the 1250s. He was clearly anxious from the outset to get control of the infant queen and of her marriage; by the Treaty of Salisbury, made in 1289 between representatives of Edward, of Eric of Norway and of the Scots 'saving always the liberty and honour of Scotland' it was agreed that 'the good people of Scotland, before they receive the Lady [Margaret was to be placed it appears into Edward's hands rather than into those of the Scots] shall give sufficient and good surety that they will in no wise marry the aforesaid Lady *save with his ordinance, will and counsel* [my italics] and with the assent of the king of Norway, her father'.[3] On 28 August 1290, the very day on which he was confirming the Treaty of Birgham, in which the detailed conditions for the marriage were set out, Edward appointed his friend Antony Bek, Bishop of Durham as lieutenant of Margaret and the young Edward, who were of course not yet married, 'to reform and set to rights the aforesaid realm (of Scotland) in conjunction with the remaining guardians'.[4] This already showed a tendency to try to dominate the Scots, a tendency which could only increase when his infant son became its king, whatever 'guarantees' had been offered in the Treaty of Birgham made in July 1290.

All these careful plans were overtaken by the death of Margaret in the autumn of 1290, in Orkney, on her way from

Norway, presumably to England, as had been provided by the Treaty of Salisbury.[5] This left the Scottish succession in total doubt. There had been some question over Margaret's succession in 1286. It was possible that Alexander's widow, his second wife Yolande of Dreux, whom he had married only five months before, might yet bear a son; but nevertheless a parliament soon after Alexander's death had accepted Margaret's succession and appointed six 'guardians' to rule, presumably till she came of age.[6] Even so, there were signs of possible trouble in the south-west, where Robert Bruce, the future competitor, and his son, the Earl of Carrick, father of the future king, seized royal castles at Dumfries and Wigtown, and the Balliol castle at Buittle in Kirkcudbrightshire.[7] We know far too little about this incident. It was ominous, however, for Bruce and Balliol were both descended from daughters of David Earl of Huntingdon, a brother of William the Lion. In default of more direct heirs, and the only one now left was the infant Margaret, they were certain to be the leading contenders for the throne. They were also rivals in the south-west, where the Bruces had held Annandale since the twelfth century, and now also Carrick, through the marriage of the younger Bruce to its heiress; while John Balliol had inherited from his mother the lordship of Galloway. The action of the Bruces looks like a pre-emptive strike to strengthen their position against Balliol. The problem was apparently resolved for the time being, though we do not know how; but after Margaret's death, the threat of civil war between the rivals was serious.

In that situation it was only natural that those most concerned for peace should have sought the support and intervention of Edward I. A letter survives from William Fraser, Bishop of St Andrews and one of the Guardians of Scotland, telling Edward of the rumours of her death, and asking him, if they should be true, to come at least to the Borders in order to prevent the outbreak of civil war which might threaten.[8] According to Fraser's account, various nobles were gathering their troops. The interregnum in any case gave

Edward an unprecedented opportunity to assert his authority, an opportunity which he did not fail to take up. If he believed he was overlord, he had to assert the position or lose it for himself and his heirs for ever. Considerations of diplomatic tact could not weigh with Edward in such a situation. He had campaigned for years at vast expense to assert the authority he claimed over Wales; there was no chance he would do less over Scotland.

Edward must have learned of the situation in Scotland in October 1290; by the end of the month he was already planning to go to Scotland, but all his plans were disarranged by the death of Queen Eleanor on 28 November, and after her funeral Edward went into retreat till late January. Once he resumed business, there was much to do before he could formally open proceedings to deal with the situation in Scotland; but by the beginning of May, a parliament was assembled at Norham to resolve the problem of the Scottish succession.[9] To it, in some way which we do not know, claimants to the vacant throne were invited to submit petitions as 'competitors'. Eventually thirteen did so.

When proceedings opened, Edward at once revealed his essential position. On 10 May, at Norham, Roger Brabazon, one of his justices, insisted that Edward's position as overlord must be accepted.[10] To this the Scots (unfortunately we do not know who represented the Scots: presumably the Guardians, perhaps among others) asked for delay to prepare a reply, which was, it seems, grudgingly granted; but the reply, when it came, was dismissed as 'nothing to the purpose' (see below) and Edward went on to extract recognition of his claims to overlordship from all the competitors. That achieved, Edward went to great lengths to reach a just and lawful decision. Many of the claims were formal, entered only for the sake of record, since they were clearly weak at this point. The three serious competitors were Robert Bruce, lord of Annandale, John Balliol, who held the lordship of Galloway, and John Hastings, all three descended from different daughters of David Earl of Huntingdon; while there was a fourth, Florence, Count of

Holland, descended from a sister of William the Lion, who tried to set aside the claims of Bruce, Balliol and Hastings on the ground that Earl David had resigned all rights to the throne. Edward took much time and trouble to resolve these difficult issues, and especially to allow Count Florence the chance to support his case, if he could do so. In the end, Florence failed to produce the vital document; and judgment was given by a body of 'auditors' of whom forty were nominated by Bruce, forty by Balliol, and twenty-four by Edward himself. There is nothing to suggest that Edward, having had his position accepted by *all* competitors, was affected by anything save a consideration of the law: there were very good legal arguments to support Balliol's claim. Inevitably, however, he had formally to swear fealty to Edward before he could be inaugurated as king on 30 November 1292. On 26 December following, as King of Scots, Balliol did homage to Edward as 'superior and direct lord of the kingdom of Scotland'.[11]

What effect had these proceedings on the Scottish sense of a distinct identity? How did the Scots react to Edward's claims?

A disputed succession was an incalculable disaster. Scotland had last experienced it in the 1090s when the brother and the offspring of the two marriages of Malcolm Canmore struggled for the kingdom. Did any Scot in 1290 recall that the ending of that dispute was the imposition of Edgar as king with the aid of William Rufus, aid which seems to have involved recognising his overlordship? The situation in 1290 threatened civil war between Bruce and Balliol who were apparently massing their forces. To the Bishop of St Andrews when he wrote to Edward with news of the situation, the English king was the only hope of peace. Bishop Fraser may well not have been alone in this view. The Scots in 1290 needed all the support they could get to maintain the peace; hence it was not easy for them to offer firm resistance to Edward's claims.

Unfortunately, we have no very clear record of the attitude of the Scots at Norham, or even of who exactly was involved on the Scottish side. The 'Great Cause', as Edward's handling of the Scottish case has ever since been known, is recorded in great detail; but the records are all from the English side and there are signs that they do not present the Scottish position at all adequately. The Scots seem mainly to have been represented, as one would expect, by the magnates who were presumably those who sought the adjournment already mentioned to prepare a reply to Edward's claim to suzerainty. The roll of Andrew de Tange, the later of the two elaborate English records of the proceedings, says that, when asked for their reply 'the Scottish nobles and prelates ... remained silent, and said, presented, showed or proposed nothing to the purpose'.[12] The account given in this notarial instrument, which was only compiled in the reign of Edward II, is hardly complete: though it was not recorded in the official texts, a copy of a response seems to have been preserved, with other material relevant to English claims, in the Exchequer, and a transcript (probably made in 1400, and now Glasgow University Library MS Gen 1053) came to notice in the present century. Among other texts it includes a response of '*la bone gens descoce*' (the good people of Scotland) with no indication as to who these 'good people' were: another name for the magnates, perhaps, or some wider group? We simply do not know. But this response was actually very much to the purpose: they declined to answer Edward's demand because, Scotland being without a king, they had no power to respond to his claims; when a king was chosen, he would be able to do whatever right and justice demanded.[13] Was it this that made Edward turn to the competitors and get their recognition? This move must have taken the wind from the sails of any Scottish protesters, even if it was clever rather than just, for it ignored the possibility that others than the king might be concerned in the rights of the kingdom of Scotland. But then the Scottish response had laid itself open to such a riposte.

It is hard on this evidence to know with clarity what was the attitude of the 'good people of Scotland' or where we should turn to find it out. The negotiations with Edward for Margaret's marriage clearly reveal an anxiety to preserve the identity, rights and customs of Scotland (the Treaty of Birgham explicitly guarantees that 'the rights, laws, liberties and customs of the kingdom of Scotland ... shall be wholly and inviolably preserved for all time'); but they are obviously negotiations for what is seen as a desirable solution. The Scots had, so far as we can tell, welcomed the backing they received from Henry III in resolving the conflicts during the minority of Alexander III; they seem to have been equally ready to turn to Edward I. By Norham, they are clearly uncomfortable with Edward's demands for overlordship, but their answer, if we accept the curiously surviving text, hedges the question. It is not a forthright rejection. And once the competitors had agreed to accept Edward's claims, there is no further sign of Scottish hesitation. After all, if they wanted to get a king without a civil war, this was clearly the best way to get one. Claims to overlordship had been around for a long time; if it was uncomfortable to have formally and explicitly to accept them, perhaps it was inevitable and perhaps better than civil war. In the proceedings of 1290–2 there is no contemporary sign of the Scottish sense of English aggression which is so characteristic of later Scottish accounts of these events; that sense was the effect of later events, even if not much later ones. The proceedings of 1290 show a sense of Scottish identity, present but not extensively articulated in a situation where the Scots had a very difficult problem to solve.

It did not take long for something to go very wrong indeed, and for this the blame must lie with Edward I. He faced very serious problems which had nothing to do with Scotland. Troubles in Gascony, and raids by French privateers in the Channel, led to open war with France; while a rising against English authority broke out in Wales. These difficulties explain some of the pressures which he put on Scotland, when, in the end, he called for military support by the Scots in his wars. But beyond that, he totally misjudged what would be the Scottish reaction to his interpretation of his position as 'lord superior'. Once Balliol had performed homage and fealty, Edward had an unequivocal admission from the King of

Scots that he, Edward, was feudal superior of Scotland. Almost at once, in what Professor Barrow has described as a 'test case', he entertained an appeal by Roger Bartholomew, a burgess of Berwick against judgments given by the Guardians. Five other Scots and three subjects of the King of England subsequently took appeals to Edward, and, ultimately in 1293, King John Balliol was forced to appear before the English parliament. He had to admit Edward's jurisdiction, which followed inevitably from his admission of Edward's superiority in 1291 and his performance of homage and fealty in 1292. The terms of the treaty of Birgham, which guaranted the independence of Scotland, had been superseded by the admissions of Balliol and the other competitors; and as the pressures built up on Edward in the middle years of the decade, there followed in 1294 demands for military service in Edward's continental wars.[14]

However, Scottish resistance did not depend on Balliol alone. Professor Barrow has emphasised the existence in these years, especially since 1286, of a sense of the 'community' of Scotland, accentuated no doubt by the need of the nobles to act on their own collectively in the interests of Scotland. It may not be a coincidence that it is just at this time, in John Balliol's reign, that we first have fragmentary records of a Scottish parliament. Something of the kind certainly existed earlier, as it had for some time in England; but it is in the records of Balliol's reign that we can see the parliament acting, as it did in England, as an ultimate court in which the king could dispense justice not available otherwise.[15] Little attention has been given to this, because the Scottish parliament never acquired the overwhelming political importance that its sister institution in England did; but it certainly existed from the late thirteenth century as an assembly of the leading landowners and eventually the 'lairds', in so far as they, the Scottish equivalent of English gentry, attended. Scotland never adopted the English practice of electing representatives of the local communities, though representatives of the burghs were summoned from the fourteenth century, probably originally

78

because of the need for taxation to raise the payments required under the terms of the eventual peace with England in 1328 and for the ransom of David II in 1357 from his captivity in England. The lack of more regular parliamentary taxation in Scotland probably explains the small part which parliament played in Scottish political life. More important, at many points, was to be the 'Council General', a body, like the English 'Great Council', consisting only of the greater landowners, and more easily summoned than parliaments. In Balliol's reign, however, these developments were still in the future; but the emergence of a parliament may help to provide a context for the forceful action which the Scottish nobles took in the face of Edward I's demands. King John himself was apparently prepared to accept Edward's calls for military service, but was confronted by a baronial revolt, a Scottish replica of 1258 in England. A baronial council effectively took control, defied Edward, and actually made an alliance against him with Philip IV of France![16] We know far too little about this episode. Needless to say, it was something which Edward was not prepared to tolerate: in 1296 he abandoned everything else, invaded Scotland, demanded unequivocal submission from all Scottish nobles he could seize; and forced Balliol's humiliating resignation in Stracathro churchyard. Edward had entered upon direct rule and Balliol was removed to captivity in England.[17]

This presented enormous problems for the Scots. For one thing, resistance to Edward was clearly hazardous. He had already shown in Wales how he responded to what he regarded as treasonable actions: Dafydd, Llywelyn's brother, had perished in public agony. Some Scots who resisted in the end fared no better. Further, the conflicts over the succession in 1290–1 had not necessarily been resolved. There had been threats of civil war then; was there now to be united resistance? Those who resisted now under William Wallace and Andrew Murray in 1297 and under various successions of Guardians for some years, took the line that John Balliol was still king; his enforced surrender was invalid, and documents continued to be issued in his name. But Balliol himself had faced baronial opposition and in 1298, while still in captivity in England, was prepared to issue a document confirming explicitly and formally that 'he found in the men of that realm [Scotland] such malice, deceit, treason and treachery, arising from their malignity, wickedness and stratagems ... that it is not his intention to enter or go into the realm of Scotland at any time to come, or to interfere in any way with it ... or ... to have anything to do with the Scots'.[18] This declaration was obviously made in an attempt to secure his release from English captivity (he was in fact released into papal custody in France in 1299); but even so, Balliol was clearly not an entirely satisfactory focus for a national resistance!

Yet resistance there was and not solely by the nobility. In the summer of 1297, there were a number of scattered risings in the south of Scotland, not all of which achieved much. But under Wallace, the Scots managed to reduce the English administration to desperation. The Treasurer, Cressingham, complained that no revenues could be collected. A separate rising in the north under Andrew Murray quickly eliminated the English garrisons around the Moray Firth. When Wallace and Murray joined forces, they were able, in September, to rout the English army under Warenne at Stirling Bridge. Professor Barrow has convincingly argued that these risings were supported by most of the Scottish nobles who could extricate themselves from the English grip, and even more by goodly numbers of the lesser gentry and commoners, both of Moray and of the southern parts of the country.[19] They are strong evidence for a sense of Scottish identity among a wide sector of the community, determined to resist English authority to the utmost.

Nor was the effort abandoned after Edward's merciless victory at Falkirk in 1298. The Scottish reaction was to continue resistance for at least five years under a succession of noble Guardians, a reversion to the constitutional arrangements of the interregnum. Edward's concern of course was to enforce the submission of as many of the Scottish nobles as he could, and it is not surprising that some hesitated to resist or gave up under pressure. Robert Bruce, the grandson of the competitor and since 1292 Earl of Carrick, might reasonably have felt that Balliol's claim was now disposed of, and that his own might come forward; the continued formal loyalty of the Scottish leaders to a deposed king who wished to have nothing more to do with them must have, at the least, irked Bruce. Yet he remained one of the leaders on the Scottish side until 1302, when he made his peace with Edward, at a time when a Balliol restoration still seemed possible. By 1304, however, he had made a secret 'band' (alliance) with William Lamberton, Bishop of St Andrews, later to be a leading figure on the side of Scottish independence. As at many other points in these confused times, we know much less than we would like of what was happening. The Balliol party had been finally crushed when Edward took Stirling Castle in 1304, and in the following year, Wallace, almost the last Scot to remain in resistance was captured and executed. Towards the end of 1305 Bruce may have felt the time was ripe for a new rising. He may have thought that Edward himself could not long survive. For whatever reasons, Bruce abandoned the English side, and apparently tried, in a meeting at Dumfries with John Comyn of Badenoch, to win over the powerful Comyn family, leaders of what had been the Balliol party, with whom Bruce's relations had often been difficult. When negotiation failed, Bruce resorted to murder, whether intentionally or not; and having thus taken the irretrievable step, pressed on at once, as he had probably planned, to claim the throne and to be crowned at Scone at Easter 1306.[20]

Even then, it was some years before Bruce had really established himself against his own enemies, now including the whole Comyn family who were enraged by his murder of their head. Edward's death in 1307 left Bruce free to deal with his enemies in Scotland. From 1309 onwards, he was increasingly secure: the power of the Comyns was finally destroyed by his victory over another John Comyn, the Earl of Buchan, at Inverurie in 1308. His own supporters, notably

James Douglas, the son of a determined opponent of Edward I in 1296, and Thomas Randolph, Bruce's nephew, were advancing steadily in power and influence. English power was reduced to scattered garrisons: most, except Jedburgh and Berwick in the far south, were reduced by 1314 when the victory of Bannockburn obtained the vital position of Stirling and left Bruce seemingly triumphant.

Yet all was still not secure. Bruce made great efforts to reconcile everyone he could after Bannockburn; and on the surface he succeeded; yet the rifts which went back to the disputed succession in the 1290s were not yet healed. A number of nobles had failed to make their peace with Bruce after Bannockburn and went into exile to become a group known as 'The Disinherited', who were to lead a movement for the restoration of John Balliol's son Edward after Bruce's death. There were some of doubtful loyalty left in Scotland, as emerged in the puzzling 'conspiracy' revealed in 1320, led nominally by William de Soules, the hereditary Butler of Scotland, a conspiracy which Bruce was able firmly to suppress.[21] Within Scotland, Bruce remained dominant until his death in 1329; but the war with England was only brought to an end by the treaty made at Edinburgh in 1328, and confirmed at Northampton in May of the same year. By it, Bruce's position as King of Scots was at last recognised, in return for a 'contribution for peace' of £20 000, and Scotland was to be 'separate in all things from the kingdom of England, assured for ever of its territorial integrity, to remain for ever free and quit of any subjection, servitude, claim or demand'.[22]

Bruce survived this triumph for little more than a year, to be succeeded by a child of five, David II, the son of his old age. He in turn was rapidly confronted by a new English threat from Edward I's grandson, Edward III, who had just seized power from his mother and her lover Roger Mortimer in 1330, and was anxious to establish his personal authority. He tried first by proxy, allowing John Balliol's son Edward to attempt a private-enterprise restoration with the help of the 'Disinherited' who had supported Edward III's own coup in

1330. For a moment, with the remarkable victory at Dupplin Moor near Perth in 1332, it seemed to have worked; but Balliol's effort soon collapsed and in 1333 Edward III took a hand himself, winning the decisive victory of Halidon Hill just north of Berwick. This restored English control of Berwick, which had been taken by Bruce in 1318, and also restored Balliol to the Scottish throne as vassal to Edward. The whole of southern Scotland, including Edinburgh, was conceded to Edward III as the price of this support; and garrisons under English commanders in support of Edward Balliol were established at Stirling, Perth, Cupar in Fife, and elsewhere.

This brought into the open the hidden uncertainties in the Scottish position, which had been suppressed by Bruce's own personality. In 1334, David II took flight to France, where he stayed at Château Gaillard till 1341. Most prominent nobles made their peace with Edward III: in the autumn of 1335 it seems that even Robert Steward, the future Robert II, was on the brink of a settlement. In that year, Edward III came to the verge of achieving what had eluded his grandfather – the final conquest of Scotland. In the latter part of 1335, the Scots were without a Guardian. Only a handful of guerilla fighters remained in the field.

Three things preserved Scottish independence. First, a victory in December 1335, at Culblean in Aberdeenshire, by Andrew Murray, the son of the victor of Stirling Bridge, over David de Strathbogie, one of the leading supporters of Balliol, a victory which he followed up two years later with a number of local triumphs which removed English power north of the Tay. Secondly, and most importantly, Edward's almost total involvement in France from 1337 onwards. Finally, in 1338 the celebrated defence of Dunbar Castle, since 1335 one of the centres of Scottish resistance in the south, by 'Black Agnes', the wife of Patrick earl of Dunbar, a resistance which seems to have done much to break the morale of the remaining English garrisons. All was not yet over: Andrew Murray, Guardian since the end of 1335 or early 1336, died in 1338, to be replaced by the much less capable Robert Steward, who spent a long time in recovering Perth in 1339. Edinburgh and Roxburgh were recovered by others in 1341, and Stirling, finally, surrendered in 1342.[23] In 1341, Bruce's son David II, now aged 17, returned from France to assume the throne.

Scotland's position was again put in some doubt, however, when, in 1346, David II intervened in the Hundred Years' War with a raid on Northern England, and was captured at the battle of Neville's Cross, just outside Durham. He remained a prisoner in England till 1357, and parts of southern Scotland were re-occupied by the English. This was, however, a much less serious threat than that in the 1330s: raids again wracked the Borders, parts of which were returned to English control, abbeys were sacked, and in 1355 a raid reached as far as Haddington; but government continued, even if falteringly, in the absence of the king; the existence of the country was not in serious doubt.

Edward III, however, put pressure on his captive to concede an English succession: David himself had no direct heir and in response to Edward's pressure he put forward the idea that he might be succeeded, not by the Steward, but by a younger son of Edward III;[24] this seems to have been acceptable to Edward, but was rejected at a parliament in Scotland which David was temporarily released to attend. In the end David was released in 1357 by a ransom treaty which conceded simply a truce. From then on, England had perforce recognised the existence in practice of an independent Scotland; Edward III had not given up the claims to overlordship but it was obvious that they could not be enforced.

This was profoundly unsatisfactory, storing up trouble for the future when Henry VIII, in the sixteenth century, resurrected these antiquated claims. It prevented any real and settled notion of peace with England. Intermittent war continued on the Borders, ensuring that neither English nor Scottish kings could really control their subjects there; and ensuring also that dissident Scottish nobles, such as the Earl of March in the early fifteenth century, or the Earl of Douglas after 1455, could always find a base in England, even if not

84

much in the way of help. The failure to reach a proper settlement in the mid-fourteenth century destabilised the Borders for two centuries and more. It also added a long-standing hostility between England and Scotland to the hostility between England and France, both disastrous after-effects of Edward III's diplomatic failures of the 1350s. The consequences of both were still clearly visible in the eighteenth century.

The identity of Scotland, however, was no longer in question. Indeed, the two centuries of recurrent warfare begun by Edward I in 1296 led to a much more clearly defined sense of a Scottish national identity. This was articulated first at the level of diplomatic arguments, particularly before the papacy in the late thirteenth and early fourteenth centuries. These ideas were later developed, in Scotland, to produce a written national history which created a past stretching far back into antiquity, all concentrated on establishing a sense of Scottish identity in opposition to the English threats. This was to play a significant part in the interpretation of Scottish history in the political revolutions of the seventeenth century and for long after.

The first beginnings of this elaborated theory of Scottish national identity appear when the Scots succeeded in persuading Boniface VIII in 1299 to call on Edward I to abandon his attempt to dominate Scotland; or, if he claimed any right over that country, to submit his case to papal judgment. Boniface's justification for this was the surprising claim that 'from ancient times the realm of Scotland belonged rightfully, and is known still to belong, to the Roman church'.[25] When Boniface's bull eventually reached Edward at Sweetheart Abbey in 1300, he saw that some response was necessary. Yet it placed Edward in a difficulty. From his point of view, Scotland was a purely internal matter, and the papacy had no right to interfere. The Scottish approach to Boniface presumed Scotland's independent existence, which Edward denied. Yet not to reply put him in danger of papal sanctions; so after much consultation, he produced a complex answer.

One part was a protest from over a hundred English barons insisting that they would not tolerate any submission by Edward to unjust papal claims;[26] another, a letter from himself informing the Pope of the 'true' situation, namely that Scotland had from earliest antiquity been subject to English overlordship. He based this case ultimately on Geoffrey of Monmouth's *History of the Britons*, in which there was an account of the division of Britain between the three sons of the alleged original settler, the Trojan Brutus.[27] This excursion into mythical history gave the Scottish delegation at Rome the chance to produce their reply. Naturally enough they passed as lightly as they could over Boniface's radical claim that Scotland belonged to the papacy; but firmly dismissed the relevance of Edward's claim, since whatever had happened between Brutus's sons, the ancient Britons had been succeeded by the Romans, the English, the Danes and eventually 'William the Bastard and his adherents from whom, rather than the Britons, this king is descended'.[28] The Scottish delegation also produced a counter-version of the origin of the Scots, whom they asserted to be descended from one Scota, a daughter of the Pharaoh who was drowned in the Red Sea in the time of Moses! We know of these arguments because the documents connected with this pleading survived in Scotland and were eventually transcribed into a fifteenth-century history written by Walter Bower, Abbot of Inchcolm, to which we will be returning later.[29] At the time, the Scots may have persuaded the Pope. John Balliol, who had in 1299 been transferred by Edward into papal custody in France, was released in 1301, to remain in France for the rest of his life.[30] Edward I, however, showed no sign of giving up his attempts to conquer Scotland and, before long, Boniface VIII quarrelled with Philip IV of France, the ally of the Scots and host to the exiled Balliol. Hence, Boniface seems from 1302 to have become less sympathetic towards the Scottish case. None the less, the Scots had started what was to be a long and productive line of argument.

Robert Bruce was clearly aware of the necessity of putting his case across in an articulate way. In 1309 he got the leaders of the Scottish church, in a parliament at St Andrews, to elaborate a justification for his kingship as a defence against English threats. 'The people' runs this declaration, '... seeing the kingdom of Scotland ... ruined and reduced to slavery [by Edward I] ... and given up to the spoiler ... agreed upon the said Lord Robert, the King who now is, in whom the rights of his father and grandfather to the foresaid kingdom, in the judgment of the people, still exist and flourish entire; and with the concurrence and consent of the said people he was chosen to be king ... and with him the faithful people of the kingdom will live and die as with one who, possessing the right of blood, and endowed with other cardinal virtues, is fitted to rule and worthy of the name of King ... since ... by repelling injustice, he has by the sword restored the realm thus deformed and ruined'.[31]

Later, Robert I in his turn, became involved in arguments with the papacy, because a new pope, John XXII, elected in 1316, was anxious to proclaim a crusade which he saw as being prevented by needless conflicts between Christian states. Edward II took advantage of this to seek papal condemnation of those whom he regarded as rebellious Scots. Hence a succession of papal bulls and missions, all designed to bring peace between Edward and the Scots, in which Bruce tended to be regarded as the obstructor. When this reached the stage of threatened excommunication of Bruce and interdict upon his kingdom, some response became necessary. Bruce and four Scottish bishops wrote to John XXII in 1320, protesting at their treatment and insisting on their desire for peace if it could be obtained with independence; but the most lasting part of the Scottish reply was a letter from thirty-nine named Scottish barons in which they insisted that the Scots had from earliest times been unconquered and independent.

Our people ... did heretofore live in freedom and peace until that mighty prince Edward, king of the English, father of the present one, when our kingdom had no head and our people harboured no malice or treachery and were then unused to war or attacks, came in the guise of friend and ally to invade them as an enemy. His wrongs, killings, violence, pillage, arson, imprisonment of prelates, burning down of monasteries, despoiling and killing of religious, and yet other innumerable outrages, sparing neither age nor sex, religion nor order, no one could fully describe or fully understand unless experience had taught him.

But from these countless evils we have been set free ... by our most valiant prince, king and lord, the lord Robert, who, that his people and his heritage might be delivered out of the hands of enemies, bore cheerfully toil and fatigue, hunger and danger, like another Maccabeus or Joshua. Divine providence, the succession to his right according to our laws and customs, which we shall maintain to the death, and the due consent and assent of us all have made him our prince and king.... By him, come what may, we mean to stand.

Yet if he should give up what he has begun, seeking to make us or our kingdom subject to the king of England or to the English, we would strive at once to drive him out as our enemy and a subverter of his own right and ours, and we would make some other man who was able to defend us our king; for as long as a hundred of us remain alive, we will never on any conditions be subjected to the lordship of the English. For we fight not for glory, nor riches, nor honours, but for freedom alone, which no good man gives up except with his life.[32]

This letter, like the rest, was part of the planned response of the Scottish government to a threatening situation. It was, however, a literary composition of remarkable power, terse, effective in its rhetoric, and brilliantly clear in its message. This 'Declaration of Arbroath' when it became widely known in the seventeenth century, was to become a classic expression of Scottish national identity, much reprinted and quoted, even in the campaign for the election of 1992!

At the time, however, this and the other statements, like the process of 1301–2 and the church declaration of 1309, were moves in a diplomatic game. We do not know how widely they were circulated. The process of 1301–2 survives only in the fifteenth-century text already mentioned; the declaration of 1309 only exists in copies of the seventeenth and eighteenth centuries; the Declaration of Arbroath is the only one of these texts to have come down to us in a contemporary version, a 'duplicate original' now in the Scottish Record Office. This last, though it may have been seen by the barons in whose name it was issued and whose seals appear on it, seems to have attracted no special notice at the time. The only accounts to quote it are two fifteenth-century chronicles; it also appears in a collection of documents attached to some fifteenth-century manuscripts of Fordun's chronicle. The text was therefore available, but there is little sign of earlier interest in it. Scotland's eventual survival in the wars against the three Edwards suggests a sense of identity sufficient to inspire their resistance, but we have no contemporary evidence of its expression outside these very capable and professional diplomatic statements. We have to infer the sentiments of the soldiers who fought with Bruce and Douglas. We know only that they did fight, like their leaders, in circumstances when it would have been simpler and safer not to do so.

The Wars of Independence not only established a disastrous pattern of Anglo-Scottish hostility; they also changed the balance of powers within Scotland. As in England, the years of conflict produced a Border society which was perforce self-reliant and quick to act in defence of what it saw as its interests. Raiding across the Border was common and instant retaliation routine. Both sides maintained a system of 'Wardens of the Marches' who tried in times of truce to maintain peace and punish transgressions. But the office of warden often served merely to strengthen the authority of those already powerful in the area, such as the earls of Douglas and Angus; and it was hard for anyone outside to control what went on in the Borders. Isolated valleys and a pastoral society much given to cattle reiving created an almost insoluble problem. Even as late as the sixteenth century, the then king, James V, had to depend on fierce raids to repress those whom he regarded as lawless brigands, rather than on a settled and regular system of law enforcement.[33] The ballad 'Johnie Armstrang' is based on one such raid by James V in 1530, in which the notorious reiver was hanged; but the ballad sees it all from Armstrang's side:

> To seik het water beneith cauld ice,
>   Surely it is greit folie –
> I have asked grace at a graceless face,
>   But there is nane for my men and me.

The ballad ends with a lament:

> John murder'd was at Carlinrigg,
>   And all his gallant companie;
> But Scotland's heart was ne'er sae wae,
>   To see sae mony brave men die –
> Because they saved their countrey deir
>   Frae Englishmen! Nane were sae bauld
> Whyle Johnie lived on the Border syde,
>   Nane of them durst cum neir his hauld.[34]

Raiding and cattle stealing could easily be seen as upholding the interests and identity of Scotland; and the king's 'justice' as savage repression of a free but fundamentally loyal society.

The wars had also served in other ways to weaken the authority of the crown. Kings of Scots in the thirteenth century may not have enjoyed enormous wealth or any very elaborate system of government, but their authority extended over the whole area between the Border with England and the Highland line. Medieval kingship depended on the personal presence of the king, and we can see from the places in which they issued charters (the 'place-dates' of the charters) that the kings of the twelfth and thirteenth centuries regularly visited all of lowland Scotland and the Borders.[35]

The Wars of Independence changed that. Robert Bruce was inevitably dependent on those who supported him, especially on Sir James Douglas and Thomas Randolph. These men had risked everything for Bruce. They had to be restored to their lands, and as Douglas led in the recovery of the Borders, it was inevitable that much would be added to his ancestral lands of Douglas in Lanarkshire. Ettrick Forest and Jedburgh were only the greatest in an enormous range of gains; and the guerilla warfare of the period up to 1357 added much more to the family's possessions. The main line of the Douglases was in minority in the 1330s and 1340s, but cadet branches flourished. William Douglas of Dalkeith added the formidable position of Liddesdale to his holdings; while another, Archibald, illegitimate son of Sir James, ultimately gained a dominant position in Galloway. These developments amounted to the establishment of a Douglas predominance in the Borders, reflected in their regular appearance as wardens. It was a predominance that David II tried to resist. In 1342 he appointed Alexander Ramsay as Sheriff of Selkirk, clearly an attempt to get an energetic and loyal supporter, who had taken a prominent part in the fighting in the late 1330s and had just recaptured Roxburgh castle, into an important office in what was becoming a Douglas area. The attempt was a disaster. William Douglas of Liddesdale seized the new sheriff as he was attempting to hold court, carried him off to Hermitage Castle in Liddesdale, and let him starve to death. David proved helpless in the face of Douglas power and William Douglas emerged as sheriff of Selkirk and custodian of Roxburgh.[36] The situation in the Borders was made far worse by the unpredictable workings of an entail (a settlement on a series of heirs) of 1342 which eventually in 1388 brought all the lands of the main line of Douglas into the hands of Archibald, the illegitimate son of Sir James, since 1369 lord of

Galloway. On the death without heirs of James, the second earl, in the battle of Otterburn, Archibald successfully claimed the whole inheritance, and became the third earl. As we shall see later, it took the drastic violence of James II, plus a certain amount of internal feuding in the family, to destroy this Douglas power in 1455.

A second, to some degree rival, power in the south was achieved by Patrick Dunbar, Earl of March. He, like many others, had an ambiguous career in the 1330s, for a year or two supporting Edward III and Edward Balliol; but he slipped back opportunely in 1335 and his castle of Dunbar became one of the centres of Scottish resistance, maintaining a Scottish presence in Lothian to counter the influence of the English garrison in Edinburgh. The earldom of March remained an important power till the end of the fourteenth century, when the then earl went into exile in England after a quarrel with the Duke of Rothesay, lieutenant at that point for his father, King Robert III.

Thomas Randolph, Bruce's other leading supporter, seemed to have achieved another palatinate, much earlier than Douglas, when Bruce gave him the office of Earl of Moray in 1312, the first deliberate creation of an earldom in Scottish history. Bruce followed this with the grant of the lordship of Man. These together made an immensely powerful position, entirely newly created, and must reflect the very great trust Bruce had in Randolph. By the series of 'tailzies' (Scots for 'entails') of the crown which Bruce established in the parliaments of 1315, 1318, and probably also in the confirmation of 1326,[37] Randolph was made regent, should the heir at the time of Bruce's death be an infant, which in fact happened in 1329. He was almost the only regent in the fourteenth century to receive unqualified praise from the chroniclers. But fate, which built up the overwhelming power of the Douglases, handled the family of Randolph very differently. Thomas himself died in 1332, just before the invasion of Edward Balliol. Thomas's son, also called Thomas, was killed at Dupplin Moor a few weeks later in 1332; and the latter's brother who succeeded and took a prominent part in the 1330s when not in captivity, was himself killed at Neville's Cross in 1346, ending the male line. The earldom then went by two successive marriages to the Dunbar family and, at that point, ceased for a time to be politically important.

We can see the effect of these developments if we compare the movements of fourteenth- and fifteenth-century kings, as revealed by the places where they granted charters, with those of their twelfth- and thirteenth-century predecessors.[38] No fourteenth- or fifteenth-century king made a habit of visiting the Borders as did Alexander II and Alexander III.

The great issue for Scottish kings in the fourteenth and fifteenth centuries, then, was how to maintain their authority over a baronage which had been greatly strengthened by the events of the Wars of Independence and by the lack of royal leadership, first in the years after 1329, when Robert I was succeeded by the infant David II, born in Robert's old age, who could not himself take control till the 1340s, and subsequently when David was again out of the country, this time as a captive in England for eleven years after the disastrous battle of Neville's Cross.

5

THE NATIONAL IDENTITY

A collapse in royal authority would have been fatal to the sense of Scottish identity, for it was the crown, with the church, that had for centuries represented that identity. At times in the later fourteenth and early fifteenth centuries, the danger must have seemed real. Yet, though the crown was at times weak, enough remained of its authority to maintain the credibility of the kingdom. At the same time, the period from the 1370s to the early fifteenth century saw a remarkable literary and historical elaboration of the ideology of national identity. From 1424 onwards, there was a revival of the authority of the crown under James I and his successors; and a further elaboration of the national mythology, all reinforcing the sense of national identity which had been articulated during the Wars of Independence.

When David II was at last ransomed in 1357, he returned to a country in which royal government had been ineffective for most of his captivity. Authority had been vested in his nephew, Robert the Steward, as King's Lieutenant, though formal acts of government continued for the most part to be issued in David's name.[1] Robert was David's nephew and heir, but he was in fact eight years older than the King. He seems to have lacked the forcefulness needed to make government function. Such evidence as we have from the sheriffs' accounts recorded on the Exchequer Rolls suggests that audits were largely in abeyance during his lieutenancy: most sheriffs only rendered accounts for much of David's captivity in 1359, after the King's release,[2] when David himself managed to revitalise the administration. From then on, regular Exchequer audits restored accountability for finance; royal charters were sought and granted in increasing numbers, as we can see from the records of the Great Seal and from surviving *acta*,[3] and the King himself undertook at least one expedition to the south-west to enforce justice in person.[4]

David seems to have been able to maintain his authority, despite some baronial opposition. In 1363, he faced a serious revolt, caused, it seems, by David's intention to marry, as his second wife, Margaret Drummond, the widow of Sir John Logie. This aroused the hostility of the Steward and the Earls of Douglas and March. Yet David was able to keep the backing of some very important lesser nobles who controlled the castles of Edinburgh, Stirling and Dumbarton; and had the resources to pay for a body of troops, which proved in the event decisive.[5] He also tried quite seriously to assert his authority in the western highlands, a policy which fifteenth-century kings were to follow.[6]

His main political weakness stemmed from his marriages and his failure to produce an heir. His first Queen, Joan, the sister of Edward III, whom he married in infancy, appears to have left him after his return to Scotland in 1357; Joan went back to England and died in 1362. She had borne him no children. A mistress was murdered in 1360. His second marriage to Margaret Logie was also childless. It took place, as we have seen, in the face of baronial opposition, and seems to have continued to cause problems thereafter. In the winter of 1368–9, Queen Margaret again clashed with the Steward and was apparently responsible for his arrest and that of other members of his family. This time, however, David ceased to support his Queen, and, in the spring of 1369, attempted to divorce her. She fled abroad and appealed to the Pope, from whom she apparently received some support. David was evidently forming yet another attachment, this time to Agnes of Dunbar, when he died, apparently unexpectedly, in 1371.[7]

Government proved much more difficult for his successors. David's nephew, the Steward, who succeeded as Robert II in 1371, had never seemed a strong personality during his periods as Lieutenant for King David. In the 1350s, his policies and those of the captive David had diverged, with David, perhaps perforce, favouring a settlement with England, while the Steward continued to think of an alliance with France.[8] As we have seen, he continued to clash with David after the King's return, though his hostility proved conspicuously futile.

The evidence for Robert II's reign is sparse and often obscure. During the 1370s and early 1380s, when English government was weak and divided, the Scots seem to have recovered most of the strong points which the English still held, notably Lochmaben Castle in Annandale in 1384.[9] Only Berwick, Roxburgh and Jedburgh remained thereafter in English hands. Robert II, however, ran into trouble in the 1380s, being declared by a Council General in 1384 unable for certain causes 'to attend himself personally to the execution of justice' (he was in his late sixties at the time). His son John, Earl of Carrick, who later took the name Robert when he became king in 1390, was to administer the common law in his place. This curious and obscure arrangement remains unexplained. In 1388, John was in turn incapacitated (by a kick from a horse!). As a result, his brother, Robert Earl of Fife was made Guardian, or according to one account 'Governor', of the realm. This appointment seems for the moment to have removed power both from Robert II, who formally consented, and from his son and heir. Nevertheless, the Earl of Fife's authority was limited and made subject, for its continuation, to what would now be termed 'positive resolution' in either Parliament or Council General.[10]

These events inaugurated a very disturbed period. Robert II died in 1390 and was succeeded by his eldest son as Robert III, though the Earl of Fife continued for some time as

Guardian. He did not, however, totally exclude Robert III from power; and in the late 1390s rivalry developed between the Earl of Fife and his nephew, Robert's son, David, Earl of Carrick, both of whom Robert III raised to dukedoms in 1398: Fife became Duke of Albany and David Duke of Rothesay, this being the first time the title of duke appears in Scotland. Robert III probably hoped by this gesture to maintain his son's position while not offending Albany, but it seems only to have heightened the conflict between them. In 1399, in a Council General, Rothesay was appointed 'king's lieutenant' for three years; a period which ended with Rothesay's 'arrest' by order of Albany; and his subsequent and highly suspicious death in custody. Albany emerged as lieutenant in his place.[11]

This was not the last of the disasters for Robert III. In 1406, he tried to send his second son James, now his heir, to security in France; instead, in March of that year, James, on his way from the Bass Rock to France, was captured off Flamborough Head by English 'pirates' who handed him over to the government of Henry IV. He remained in English captivity till 1424. Robert III himself died a few weeks after hearing of his son's capture, leaving Albany acting as 'governor' till his death in 1420, when he was succeeded by his eldest son, Murdoch, second Duke of Albany.

These developments remain exceedingly obscure. At every turn we have only formal records, mainly of Councils General, and often unenlightening and puzzling accounts by later chroniclers. At least till the mid-1380s, Robert II seems to have ruled with some effect and maintained control of his barons. Thereafter age may have told. Robert III's reign seems a tale of bitter rivalries, which the King could not control; but Albany's rise to power seems never to have been very secure, and his ultimate authority as governor depended on his being able to win the backing of the very powerful Earls of Douglas and Mar. Albany held his position only at the price of sharing authority with these two who remained almost independent. Indeed, the fourth Earl of Douglas made a notable career for himself fighting for the French against Henry V, and he enjoyed trust and high position in France until his death at Verneuil in 1424. What little evidence we have of Albany's and Murdoch's governorship leaves the impression of very limited authority.[12] Their power depended on the unwillingness of the English government, especially under Henry V, to contemplate James's release.

However, because, in the 1420s, more and more Scots joined in the Hundred Years' War on the French side, the Dukes of Bedford and Gloucester, who dominated English government in France and at home during the minority of the infant Henry VI, increasingly came to see the possible advantages of releasing James I. He had grown up at the court of Henry V and had, towards the end of Henry's reign, been taken along with the English armies in France, as a means of convicting the Scots in France of treason against their own king. James seems to have admired Henry V; and there was a good prospect that, if liberated, he would discourage or prevent the Scots from engaging on the French side. His release in 1424 brought to an end the rule of the Albany Stewarts.

Yet, throughout this period, though royal authority was weakened, it was not destroyed. In the difficulties of the later part of Robert II's reign, and throughout the reign of Robert III, the formal workings of government were maintained, even if one has a sense that the powerful were hardly under control. Little if anything, for example, was done to check the lawlessness of Albany's brother, Alexander, Earl of Buchan, known to history as the 'Wolf of Badenoch' for his violence in the north in the 1390s. During the minority and captivity of James I, from 1406 to 1424, the Albanies had to share power with others, but on these terms, reasonable order was maintained. Government did not collapse.

Nor did the concept of a national identity. The period from 1370 to the 1420s saw the remarkable flowering of a national literature and history which openly emphasised as never before the notion of a Scottish identity rooted in the ancient and largely mythical past. This identity was also strongly emphasised in accounts of the recent past, and especially of the Wars of Independence.[13] Ideas which had been put forward at the turn of the thirteenth and fourteenth centuries by the clerks and diplomatic representatives of the Guardians and of Robert I were now becoming part of the general currency of Scottish history.

Their first more public expression was in the epic poem on the Wars of Independence, *The Bruce*, written by John Barbour, Archdeacon of Aberdeen, in the mid-1370s. We do not know whether this poem was inspired by Robert II, but it certainly obtained favourable recognition from him in a pension granted in 1378 to Barbour and his assignees for ever.[14] *The Bruce* is the tale of the wars from the death of Alexander III in 1286 to Bruce's death and the burial of his heart at Melrose, a tale of the determination of the English to destroy the Scottish kingdom, told to exalt Bruce and Douglas as the heroes of the Scottish nation. It laid the basis of the Scottish national myth of the wars as it has been ever since.

Only two manuscripts survive, both written late in the fifteenth century, and the poem was not printed till 1571. It was, however, clearly known to and used by Andrew of Wyntoun, the Prior of St Serf's in Loch Leven, in composing a history of Scotland in verse at the end of the fourteenth century, and by Walter Bower, Abbot of Inchcolm in the fifteenth century. To these histories we shall return later. Barbour is an important historical source as well as the literary begetter of a view of the wars which has been very influential; but the lack of surviving manuscripts of his text is an indication of how much else we may have lost.

Around the same time as Barbour wrote, one John of Fordun was compiling a history of the Scots. We know almost nothing of him except his name, which suggests that he came from the place that is now Fordoun in Kincardineshire. The mid-fifteenth-century copyist of one of the manuscripts of Walter Bower's elaboration of Fordun's work (see below), describes Fordun as a 'chaplain of the church of Aberdeen' and another, who wrote his manuscript before 1480, tells us that Fordun went to much trouble, including study visits to England, to assemble his material.[15] Like many another researcher he somewhat over-reached himself. His aim was a history of the Scots from the very beginnings, and he clearly intended to reach his own day; but like the examination candidate who runs out of time, Fordun was reduced to increasingly sketchy notes as he progressed through the middle ages, to end in the fullest version in 1384. But wherever he hoped to finish, his primary aim was fixed far in the past, to tell in detail the origin of the Scots whose identity and history he wanted to set forth.

His story is an elaboration of the brief mention of Scottish origins contained, in passing, in the Declaration of Arbroath of 1320, and in rather more detail in the Scottish arguments before Pope Boniface VIII in 1301–2; Fordun gives a detailed account of the doings of Scota, who was merely named in the earlier arguments, and her Greek husband Gaythelus; of their flight from Egypt after her father's death in the Red Sea in the time of Moses, and of their eventual settlement in Spain. His first book continues with the journeyings of their descendants to Ireland and their ultimate settlement, centuries later, in Scotland. In later books he describes the subsequent history of the Scots and of the Picts, but with increasing difficulty as he is confronted with the conflicting accounts which he found in classical historians, in Bede's Ecclesiastical History, in the surviving lists of Pictish and Scottish kings, and in the twelfth-century 'History of the Britons' by Geoffrey of Monmouth, which he criticises severely. Not surprisingly he found their many contradictions hard to unravel, as have many more recent historians. As he progresses, he can rely rather more on the writings of the twelfth-century English chroniclers, such as William of Malmesbury and Henry of Huntingdon; and the continental historian Vincent of Beauvais.[16] The purpose of the telling, however, is clear to any reader, and it is very much the purpose which lay behind the Declaration of Arbroath. Fordun's point is to emphasise the independent origin and continuing independence of the Scots; and how they had firmly maintained that independence against all comers, even Julius Caesar, who, Fordun asserted, contemplated the suppression of Scottish independence, but was rebuffed by the firm letter of defiance sent to him by the kings of Scots and Picts. He was in any case prevented by a revolt in Gaul from putting their capacity to the test,![17] This remarkable tale appears in a passage which is developed around Geoffrey of Monmouth's account of Caesar's dealings with the tribes of southern Britain; and is obviously intended to show how much more effective were the Scots (and their alleged allies the Picts) in resisting the Romans, than were the southern Britons. Unfortunately, it has no basis in fact, and may be Fordun's own invention. Caesar never came near what is now Scotland; and the Scots themselves did not arrive there till, at earliest, some five centuries later!

Fordun was followed in the succession of Scottish historians by a rather different writer, Andrew of Wyntoun, a canon of St Andrews who became Prior of St Serf's in Loch Leven.[18] He is believed to have been born soon after the middle of the fourteenth century,[19] and his work, *The Orygynale Cronykil of Scotland* was apparently not finished till after the death of the first Duke of Albany in 1420. Although Wyntoun's main narrative ends with the death of Robert III in 1406, he continues with an enthusiastic eulogy of Albany, ending with the hope that his son may prove as good as he was:

> Off hym ennuch I can nocht speke.
> The froit of hym God grant to be
> Sic, as in his tym wes he.[20]

Wyntoun's history, a long verse chronicle of the history of the world and Scotland from its origins, hence the 'original' in the title, is a less assertively nationalist work than either Barbour's or Fordun's, both of which he clearly knew. Wyntoun's theme is the history of the world from the creation, and Scotland figures at appropriate points only, till we reach Kenneth mac Alpin, after which the narrative deals mainly with Scottish history; but all the elements of the origin myths are there, though not exactly following the version in Fordun. When he comes to the Wars of Independence, he refers frequently to Barbour; but also follows Fordun very closely indeed in parts of the particular account he gives of Edward I's decision in favour of Balliol. Like Fordun, he attributes this decision to Edward's desire to have a more complaisant ruler in Scotland than Bruce would have been.[21]

By the time James I returned from captivity in 1424, Scotland was equipped with at least two full histories, one in Latin prose, the other in Scots verse, which traced the Scots back to their earliest and distinctive origins in the times of Moses; and with Barbour's epic glorification of the deeds of Bruce and Douglas in their struggle for independence against the attacks of Edward I and his son. This 'national literature' marks a crucial stage in the articulation of a Scottish national identity.

James's return began a period of highly autocratic Stewart rule. The newly restored king was clearly anxious to re-assert royal authority after the weakness of two successive 'governors'. He also had the model of Henry V before him, though he may have missed the point that the English king's severity could claim to be based on a firm sense of justice. James I quickly swept away the Albany Stewarts in a series of show trials and executions.[22] He tried to deal with other problems, such as the independence of the Lordship of the Isles, in similar high-handed fashion, even if less drastically. Faced with recurrent rebellion and feuding in the north, he summoned Alexander, claimant to Ross, Lord of the Isles, along with numerous other northern magnates, to a 'meeting' at Inverness in 1428, at which they were all arbitrarily seized. After this show of force, James tried to get Alexander's co-operation. He was released in the hope that he might help to restore the area to order. This failed, however, because Alexander was either unwilling or unable to play the part intended. Medieval nobles, in Scotland or elsewhere, could not always constrain unwilling supporters; and the men of

Ross and the Isles were resentful at James's attempts to curb their feuds. In 1429, James had to take the field himself and crush Alexander's forces, weakened by desertion, in a battle in Lochaber. Alexander's life was spared, but he was imprisoned in Tantallon castle. Yet even this did not achieve James's object. The Clan Donald, of which Alexander was the head, still resisted: in 1431, the Earl of Mar, given the task of dealing with their revolt, was himself routed at Inverlochy, to the north-east of Fort William; and in the end, James had release Alexander and restore him to all his positions. At this price, and after a period of imprisonment, he was now ready to co-operate. James had to accept and work with those who had power in the north.[23]

James also tried to strengthen his authority by introducing reforms in the workings of government, perhaps inspired by his observation, as a captive, of the much more elaborate structures of English government. Some of these, to which we will return, were the beginning of developments which were to be important in the future. Few had much effect at the time.

James's attention was taken up more with complex negotiations with the papacy, in which he tried to prevent what he regarded as papal interference in the workings of the Scottish church. James, like Henry V, regarded the church in his kingdom as primarily his affair, and wanted as little papal intervention as possible; he was, however, also concerned for the welfare of the church. Like Henry V in 1421, he complained of the laxity of the monastic orders. In a letter to the abbots and priors of the Benedictines and Augustinians, James demanded that they 'take care ... how the fervour of religious life can most easily be revived to its pristine state ... lest through your negligence and idleness the kings who formerly ... splendidly endowed your monasteries in times past ... may regret their munificence in erecting walls of marble when they consider how shamelessly you have abandoned the practices of your orders.' Like Henry V, James also founded a Carthusian monastery, in his case at Perth, which was to be the last monastic foundation in Scotland before the Reformation.[24]

In dealing with foreign affairs, he tried to keep up diplomatic relations both with England and France, though it was increasingly clear that he inclined to France. The English government of the minority of Henry VI had hoped, when they agreed to James's release, that they would gain an ally against France; but these hopes soon proved vain. Payments towards his ransom lapsed, something which caused deep resentment among the noble relatives of the hostages thus left languishing in England; but James wanted the money for other things. In 1436, he launched a disastrously unsuccessful attempt to recover Roxburgh castle. This humiliating failure only added to the grievances already caused by his disregard of the interests of the hostages and provoked some trouble in the parliament which met at the end of 1436.

In February 1437, this discontent culminated in James's murder by a group headed by his uncle, Walter Stewart, Earl of Atholl, the only surviving son of Robert II. The other conspirators were of much less standing, but all had particular grievances against the King, some of which went back to James's destruction of the Albanies. Several of the murderers had been long-standing servants of Dukes Robert and Murdoch, and seem to have been anxious to take even belated vengeance on the King. The conspirators presumably hoped for general support, but they made no statement of their aims, and any justifications they may have offered are not recorded. For a month the issue was in doubt, but in the end there was little backing for the murderers. James's widow, Joan Beaufort, and those around her were able to bring the assassins to trial and execution.[25] The events of 1437 should have been a warning to the Stewarts to walk warily; but they did not destroy the authority of the monarchy.

James II, however, was only seven when he succeeded; and the inevitable minority saw further rivalries, particularly within the now many-branched family of Douglas, in whose hands much of the effective power lay. In 1440 William, the young sixth earl, was arrested and executed on a charge of treason by Sir Alexander Livingston and William Lord Crighton, who at the time dominated the government being conducted on behalf of the young James II. The sources give no clear explanation of this dramatic event. The sixth earl left no offspring. His younger brother was executed with him and the title went to his much older cousin James, who became the seventh earl. The circumstances suggest that he may well have been behind the arrest and execution of his relations. Certainly he showed no sign of resentment at their deaths.[26] There were rivalries also among those, such as Livingston and Crighton, who had risen in government offices during the minority; and thus James II, when he came to exercise power on his marriage in 1449, at the age of 19, may have seen the necessity to assert himself. He began by taking control of the holders of office; but more drastically continued by trying to break the power of the Douglases. The execution of the young Earl of Douglas and his brother during the minority in 1440, may well have opened rifts in the Douglas affinity. If their uncle James, who became seventh earl on their deaths, was in any way responsible for what had happened, it would hardly be surprising that this should have alienated many of the long-standing followers of the main line of the Douglases in the south-west. His own lands were centred at Abercorn on the Forth near South Queensferry and he had no roots in traditional Douglas territory.

He died in 1443 and it was his son William, the eighth earl, who had to bear the brunt of the king's efforts to reduce the power of the family. James may well have tried to take advantage of discontent within the Douglas affinity. There are signs around 1450 of what Dr McGladdery has called 'a subtle yet concerted effort on the part of the king to entice Douglas supporters away from him [the eighth earl of Douglas] and to build up the position of trusted men in areas within or adjacent to Douglas territory'.[27] It seems that Douglas may have responded to this pressure by making a 'bond' of alliance with two other powerful nobles, the Earls of Crawford and

Ross. This aroused the King, and he summoned Douglas to a dinner at Stirling Castle in February 1452, at which he tried to persuade Douglas to break the bond. Douglas however refused point blank. James, in fury, burst out 'False traitor, since you will not, I shall!' and stabbed him.[28]

This violent reaction by a king given to high temper, showed two contrasting things. First, it revealed that the authority of the King remained high, for the remaining members of the main line of Douglas were not able to capitalise on this crime to defy him. Three years later James was able to complete their destruction at the battle of Arkinholm and the siege of Threave castle in Galloway, their last stronghold, where his artillery proved decisive. The bulk of the nobility would not take to arms against the King. Secondly, James found he had to work very hard in the months after the murder in order to win and maintain the nobles' support.[29] Support had to be sought and bought with grants: it could not simply be counted on.

One thing which perhaps helped James II's restoration of royal authority was the importance of the monarchy as a focus for the sense of Scottish identity. It can hardly be pure coincidence that the decade after the murder of James I saw the elaboration of Fordun's pioneering history into the enormously extended *Scotichronicon*, compiled by Walter Bower, Abbot of Inchcolm, a text which immediately became the basic account of Scottish history; manuscripts proliferated, and abbreviations were made, by Bower himself and others, to make the work more accessible.[30] The earliest manuscript of this history to survive, which was prepared at Inchcolm under the supervision of Bower himself, ends with the phrase 'Christ! He is not a Scot who is not pleased with this book.'[31] The last portion of the text is an extensive eulogy of 'our lawgiver king', explicitly designed to underline the contrast with the disorders of the minority which followed his death, and to encourage the young James II to emulate what Bower represents as the virtues of his father.[32] Bower is stressing both the importance of history for the sense of Scottish identity, and the importance of a strong and effective monarchy as the focus for that identity. Throughout, he follows Fordun's earlier emphasis on the Scots as free and unconquered from their ancient beginning, but carries the history on in full to the death of James I, with increasingly large additions and developments from other sources. From the Wars of Independence onwards it is effectively a new composition, though what Fordun himself wrote is normally embedded in Bower's more extensive text.

After James II began to govern in person in 1449, he certainly showed a determination to assert the royal authority, and to maintain his power. On the overthrow of the Douglases in 1455 James was able to annex their lands, a great addition to the wealth of the crown, as well as a means to reward those who had supported him in the conflicts of the years from 1452 to 1455.

He also moved, as soon as he was able, to try to recover Berwick and Roxburgh, both still in English hands. This was in part because the Earl of Douglas had been given asylum in England, though no effective backing; also because an attack on England was a way of gaining support and popularity in Scotland. His first plans for an expedition proved abortive: he could not get French support, and doubted his ability to act without it. Truces were therefore made with England and renewed for the time being. But the Lancastrian defeat at Northampton in 1460 so weakened Henry VI's authority that James was at last able to launch an attack on Roxburgh.

He proved, however, too interested in the new weaponry of the age. He stood too near a cannon which exploded when it was fired and killed the King. The expedition, however, was successful, for after James's death the castle fell to his army. This ended the English occupation of Teviotdale, the last remains, save for Berwick, of the English gains in the Wars of Independence.

Another difficult minority followed for his son James III, who succeeded at the age of eight in 1460. For a time his mother, Mary of Gueldres, tried to make a settlement with the

Yorkist party, now dominant in England after the battle of Towton in 1461; her chief rival for power, Bishop Kennedy of St Andrews, continued to offer support to the defeated house of Lancaster. Kennedy's hopes for a Lancastrian restoration, however, collapsed with the failure of a Scottish attempt to capture Norham castle, just on the English side of the Border, in 1463. It was, in the end, Mary's policy which, long after her death in 1463, provided the model for her son's efforts to achieve a settlement with the Yorkist Edward IV in the 1470s.[33] Kennedy's death in 1465 was followed in 1466 by the dramatic seizure of the King and power by the Boyd family, prominent Ayrshire landowners, with the support of at least two Border lairds, Hepburn and Ker. This coup, which looked like a return to the troubles of James II's minority, when Crighton and Livingston were rivals for the control of the young King, collapsed in a counter-coup in 1469. This was easily and effectively carried through by James himself, who seized power at the age of seventeen.

In the 1470s, James made serious efforts to reach a settlement with England. He was successful for a short time in 1474, but it was a policy that provoked much resistance. It was probably around 1474 that 'Blind Hary', of whom we know next to nothing, produced *The Wallace*.[34] This poem, developed from Barbour's *Bruce*, returned to the theme of the Wars of Independence, apparently as an expression of hostility to the King's policies. Hostility to England, by now traditional, was still too strong for any attempt at formal reconciliation.

James had trouble too with his own family. His brothers, the Earls of Albany and Mar were accused of treason in 1479: Albany fled into exile while Mar was executed. A major revolt in 1482 resulted in James being held in captivity in Edinburgh for a short time. The disaffection of his son and heir in 1488 contributed to a second revolt in that year, as a result of which James himself was murdered, by an unknown assailant, after his defeat in the battle of Sauchieburn. None of these events are well recorded, and it is hard to be certain what lay behind them. But it is clear at least that James III was not one of the more successful of the Stewart kings.

His defeat brought to the throne his young son James IV, who, after this unhappy start, proved himself perhaps the most effective of his family to date.[35] He was able to win the support of the nobility, whom he handled shrewdly and carefully; he was able to complete the efforts of his predecessors to win control of the Lordship of the Isles; he also for much of his reign showed himself adept at foreign policy, gaining a peace with England in 1502 and the marriage to Margaret Tudor in the following year, which eventually brought his great-grandson to the throne of England in 1603. Yet this peace, described by Dr Macdougall as 'even more brittle than its predecessor of 1474' lasted only a few years.[36] Before long James was showing signs of returning to the traditional line of the French alliance, despite every diplomatic effort that could be made by Henry VII and Henry VIII. In 1508 Thomas Wolsey reported to his master Henry VII on an embassy to Scotland, saying that not only was James determined to ally with France, but that all his subjects, except the Queen and the Bishop of Moray were calling on him daily to do so.[37]

Eventually, James took the long-expected step and in 1512 agreed to join the French league against Henry VIII. His weakness as a general in the battle of Flodden in 1513 resulted in one of the greatest disasters in Scottish history. He and many of his leading nobles were killed. Yet the policy which led to this, and the campaign itself, was one of the most enthusiastically supported actions by a king of Scots since the Wars of Independence!

Since 1424, all the kings had been strong personalities, and for the most part effective, despite the problems of recurrent minorities. These minorities meant that each king in turn had to start by establishing his personal authority. It was fortunate that each proved able to do so, for Scottish government still depended very heavily on the personal initiative of the king.

Scotland had been very late in developing the sort of formalised administration that England and many other European countries had long possessed, which reinforced their kings' personal authority and the sense of a national identity by the authority of a regularly functioning admin- istration. Scotland hardly needed a system as elaborate as that of England, but there are signs in the fifteenth century of developments towards a more settled and less personal style of government. As late as the fourteenth century, royal admin- istration was still very simple in its outlines. The king's chapel issued his letters; his chamberlain handled the royal finances. There was no professional central court: local justice was handled by sheriffs, who were local landowners and often hereditary, and by baronial justiciars, who had authority in particular areas, or occasionally by the king in person. David I in the 1130s and 1140s may or may not have regularly allowed himself to be deflected from a hunt, as Ailred described him as doing in his eulogy of that king, to do justice to a poor man who appealed to him[38] – such stories are part of the mythology of medieval kingship, as we may see if we read Joinville's account of Louis IX doing justice with similar informality – but Scottish kings remained liable in the fourteenth century to do justice in person or to be upbraided for not doing so. David II, after his return from captivity in 1357, responded to complaints of disorder during his absence by himself setting out on a justice ayre (Scots for 'eyre', a judicial circuit). We know from Bower's chronicle that one criminal was caught, tried and hanged on the spot, showing that the king's justice, if he happened to be present, could be swift and effective.[39] The whole scale and structure of government in fourteenth century Scotland is more like that of England in the reign of Henry I than at any time after the great structural developments there in the twelfth century. The change for Scotland came in the fifteenth century.

This may to some extent have been the result of James I's experience of the much more elaborate English system during the years of his captivity from 1406 to 1424, and especially during the years when he was allowed to watch Henry V's government in action. As we have seen, he may well have regarded Henry V as a model of kingship. It can hardly be a coincidence that James founded a Carthusian house at Perth in 1429, seeing that Henry also founded a house of that order at Sheen in 1414; and his determined strike against the Albany Stewarts may have been inspired by the strong and summary justice which he had observed, for instance, in the suppression of the Cambridge plot in 1415. In 1428 he tried to develop the Scottish parliament by replacing the general summons to the lairds by the more practical system of the election of 'commissioners' from sheriffdoms, an idea which looks like an adaptation of the English practice of elected representatives from the shires.[40] Little seems to have come of this: the practice, if ever adopted at all, soon lapsed.

In more general ways the much more systematic English administration may have suggested reforms. There is little evidence in Scotland of formal sessions of a King's Council before the fifteenth century, through the witness lists of royal charters suggest that prominent nobles and officials often met with the king, and presumably discussed business with him. Under James I, we find signs of special 'sessions' of the Council in Parliament to do justice. This may have been suggested by English practices; these sessions continued during the century until, by the 1460s, the records of their proceedings, as Lords Auditors of Causes and Complaints, are sufficient to be printed as a separate series. Though still formally part of the proceedings of Parliament, these sessions had become in effect a court of law distinct from the Council as a political body. We know too little of the details to be sure exactly when or how this came about: it seems likely that the 1450s were an important stage in the process. By 1532, these sessions of the Council became the professional and paid 'Court of Session' formally established by James V in that year.

Within the king's chapel there was developing a system of separate offices of the signet, privy seal and great seal, and a 'course of the seals', each warranting the next, in similar

111

fashion to the practice of the English Chancery. By the end of the century, Scottish government is acquiring a much more formal guise than it had had in the fourteenth.

By the end of the fifteenth century, there had been a great elaboration of the national origin myth and of the nationalistic anti-English Scottish history in the writing of Walter Bower and his abbreviators, and of the myths of the Wars of Independence in *The Wallace*. There was also a revived monarchy, particularly under James I, James II and James IV; and a considerable development of the structure of government. The integrity and independence of Scotland were no longer in question; and it was hardly surprising that James III should have made recurrent efforts to achieve a settlement with England, for the continued hostility had little to offer either country. Yet the sense of enmity which had developed between England and Scotland in the early fourteenth century was still alive. The popularity of James IV's revival of the war in 1512–13 confirmed that the sense of Scottish identity was still overwhelmingly anti-English.

6

SCOTLAND AND CHRISTENDOM

> We beseech your holiness ... to admonish and exhort the
> king of the English ... to leave in peace us Scots who live in
> this poor little Scotland, beyond which there is no dwelling-
> place at all, and who desire nothing but our own.
>
> (The Declaration of Arbroath, 1320, addressed to
> Pope John XXII)[1]

This picture of Scotland as poor and remote, the last outpost
before the vast emptiness of the ocean, has stuck very hard. It
goes back to Tacitus who wrote of Caledonia, 'when you go
farther north you find a huge and shapeless tract of country,
jutting out towards the land's end and finally tapering into a
kind of wedge',[2] the final limit of the voyage of Agricola's
fleet. He added a vivid description of the strength and
sluggishness of the ocean and, by implication, of its danger. It
was an image which the Scots could cultivate when it suited
them, and which fitted well with the fierce nationalism which
we see in so much of Scottish literature in the two centuries
after the Wars of Independence.

Was the country, however, really so isolated? In the
beginning it was certainly not so. From earliest record
Scotland was inhabited by settlers from many regions: Ireland,
Scandinavia and, of course, the rest of Britain. With all of

these the inhabitants of Scotland remained linked and in contact.

Contacts across the Irish Sea went back before the 'Scots' came to Scotland, for it was a missionary from Cumbria, St Patrick who, legend says, first converted the Irish; and from his Irish base he wrote complaining of attacks by a king of Strathclyde against his, Patrick's, parishioners.[3] Even so early, the Irish Sea was no barrier; and certainly the later Columban monasteries at Iona and elsewhere remained in touch with their Irish origins. The best known work of early Irish art, the Book of Kells, may well be a product of Iona, whence it may have migrated to Kells from which it got its name; and much of the knowledge of these 'dark ages' in Scotland comes from Irish annals.

Scandinavian contacts are less well documented; yet it is the Icelandic sagas composed in the twelfth century and later which give us most of our information on the Norse areas and about how Scandinavian rulers involved themselves in, and tried to maintain control of, what was to be part of Scotland.

In the south, British Strathclyde extended from Cumbria to Dumbarton, while the Anglians in Northumbria reached to the Forth and perhaps beyond in the seventh century; both straddled the later Border. Specimens of Anglian art are to be found, not only at Ruthwell but also at Hoddom in Dumfriesshire as well as at Jedburgh and St Andrews. 'Pictish' art, in the north-east, is eclectic in its incorporation of motifs from earlier Anglian models;[4] while the 'hog-back' monuments at Govan church, just south of the river Clyde in the north of British Strathclyde, are memorial stones which seem to represent Norse long-houses; these may show direct Norse influence, or may reflect contacts with northern England, where there are similar Norse monuments. They now survive, along with a sarcophagus with interlace ornaments with both Pictish and Anglian elements, and crosses in Celtic style.[5] Scotland before the eleventh century was in touch with, and influenced by, many other societies.

We would like to know how far Scots travelled abroad in the period before the twelfth century, but it is hard to tell, especially because of the uncertain meaning of 'Scots' in continental sources: *Scoti*, till at least the ninth century, usually means 'Irish', as with the *Scottas* who arrived unexpectedly at Alfred's court in 891 and who are explicitly said, in the Anglo-Saxon Chronicle, to have come from Ireland.[6] We know that Macbeth visited Rome in 1050, though our chief source, the expatriate Irish recluse, Marianus Scotus, gives us no clue as to the purpose of the visit; he tells us only that Macbeth scattered alms to the poor 'like seed'.[7] This may suggest that an eleventh-century Scottish king was anxious to keep up, for instance, with Cnut who went there in 1027, but is hardly evidence for regular contact. It is interesting, however, that around the same time, the Norse Earl Thorfinn the Mighty of Orkney also visited Rome.[8] Two references in the writings of Guibert, Abbot of Nogent in north-eastern France from 1104, to the Scots, 'Bare-legged with their shaggy cloaks' and already wearing something very like a sporran, make it clear that Scottish soldiers did appear on the Continent and join in the First Crusade; though his description of them as 'a crowd of devils', attacking a novice of his monastery, suggests that they were not always welcome, even if he also recognised their 'faith and devotion'.[9]

The so-called 'Anglo-Norman Era', the period from St Margaret in the late eleventh century to the death of Alexander III in 1286, brought Scotland into much closer contact both with England and with other parts of western Europe. It brought to Scotland many, laymen and clerics alike, who had wide experience elsewhere, and often personal and family links with England and France, which all helped to integrate Scotland into the wider feudal society which dominated the north-west of the European continent.

This is particularly evident as we look at the careers of Scottish churchmen. A significant number were not by origin Scots. When Queen Margaret came to look at the Scottish church, it was its isolation that troubled her; its practices and structures were to her eyes peculiar and outdated, and she looked to England and the rest of Christendom for a remedy. She established contact with Lanfranc, Archbishop of Canterbury, a man whose experience went back to the northern Italy of the earlier eleventh century and who had taken an important part in the development of both the Norman and English churches. Her son, Alexander I, in the early twelfth century, also relied on England for the new blood which he needed for the church. His first two appointments to the see of St Andrews, Turgot and Eadmer, were both English monks. Eadmer's successor, Robert, previously Prior of Scone, was in origin a canon of Nostell, near Pontefract in Yorkshire. A significant number of later bishops of St Andrews, or those who hoped to be such, also originated outside Scotland. Among those who seem to have been 'foreigners' were John 'the Scot' (elected in 1178, though forced to concede defeat in a contested election), who, despite his name, was alleged to have been born in the county of Chester; Roger of Leicester (elected in 1189 but not consecrated until 1198), son of Robert Earl of Leicester; and William Malveisin (consecrated to Glasgow in 1200, and to St Andrews in 1202), probably of French origin.[10] The history of other dioceses would extend the list of non-Scottish bishops. The episcopate was clearly not a Scottish preserve. Of course, this was normal for the time: the Christian church was a universal institution, and there were French holders of English sees, and at least one English holder of a French see. It is not till the thirteenth century that these appointments were to be affected by more national considerations.

The new monasticism introduced by Margaret's sons brought many more outsiders and outside contacts to Scotland. As we have seen, monasteries were generally founded by a 'plantation' from an existing house elsewhere; and the relations so established were often maintained for centuries. Cistercian houses kept up particularly close contacts since their system placed daughters under the authority of the mother-houses. Rievaulx in Yorshire had both Melrose and

Dundrennan among its daughters; each in turn founded others as was the Cistercian pattern: from Melrose were established Newbattle, Kinloss, Coupar Angus and, later, Balmerino; from Dundrennan, Glenluce and ultimately Sweetheart. Thus a number of the most important Scottish abbeys were tied firmly to one of the leading Cistercian houses in northern England.

A further continental link was also established with a second French reformed order, that of Thiron, in Eure et Loire, founded in 1109 by another monk who, like the early Cistercians, was unhappy within the traditional Benedictine monasticism and sought a simpler and more basic rule of life, back to what he saw as the essentials of work and prayer rather than elaborate rituals. In the end, Thiron was eclipsed by the great success of Clairvaux under St Bernard, though it retained its own independence. But it seems to have had an early and interesting attraction for the fringe areas of Britain: around 1115, Robert fitz Martin founded from Thiron an abbey which became St Dogmael's on the Teifi in west Wales; and around the same time Earl David, who perhaps knew Robert fitz Martin at the court of Henry I, turned to the same source to found his abbey at Selkirk, later moved to Kelso, from which later was founded Lesmahagow, probably Kilwinning and Lindores, and certainly Arbroath. Thiron, however, did not maintain the tight network of the Cistercians – Kelso, though it provided the monks, specifically disclaimed any authority over Arbroath, which was founded by William the Lion in 1178 – and we do not know if the Scottish group maintained any particular links among themselves, or with their originator in France.

Beyond this, as we have seen, the twelfth century saw the idea of a universal church becoming an administrative and legal reality. Contacts between Scotland and the papacy became increasingly regular. We have seen how the Scottish church's resistance to dominance from York involved the papacy; how by the 1170s the Scottish church was seeking the backing of Alexander III against the claims and actions of

117

Henry II. In 1125 and 1138 Cardinals were accredited as papal legates to Scotland. From the pontificate of Innocent II, who died in 1143, Scottish monasteries began to get papal privileges: the first two were protections to Kelso and Newbattle; St Andrews followed under Lucius II and under Eugenius III (1145–53) papal privileges are recorded to Holyrood, Cambuskenneth, St Andrews, Jedburgh and Kelso.[11] By the mid-fifties of the twelfth century, the Scottish church was well and truly involved in dealings with the papacy. The curia was to become not just a source of legal privileges and occasional support, but by the later middle ages also a channel for preferments vital to the livelihood of countless Scottish clerics, as of those of every province of the Christian church. But in 1153, when Eugenius died, that was still far in the future.

The 'twelfth-century renaissance' provided other reasons for contacts with England and mainland Europe. The cathedral schools which emerged in the Loire valley and the Île de France rapidly joined the legal schools of Italy as centres of higher education which attracted scholars from much of western Europe. They swiftly replaced the monasteries as centres of learning in the church and providers of educated clerks and lawyers for royal administration. During the twelfth century, this produced a certain cosmopolitanism among the inevitably tiny educated élite. Becket, chancellor to Henry II and then Archbishop of Canterbury, had been trained at London, Paris, Bologna and Auxerre; while his faithful follower, John of Salisbury, who ended his career as bishop of Chartres, was educated at Paris and Chartres. The growth of English universities in the thirteenth century soon narrowed the backgrounds of most English churchmen; but Scotland had no universities until St Andrews was founded in 1411; so that those who sought advancement through higher education had no choice but to go outside Scotland. We cannot say whether any twelfth-century Scottish bishops had followed the sort of careers which helped to advance Thomas Becket and John of Salisbury. We have little idea of the educational background of any twelfth-century Scottish bishop, except that very many of them were monks. The first to be specifically designated a master was John 'the Scot' Bishop-elect (briefly) of St Andrews, and Bishop of Dunkeld from 1183; it is uncertain where he took his degree. A late tradition was that he had studied at Oxford and Paris. By the end of the thirteenth century, there is more definite information. Professor Watt has drawn attention to a group of bishops at that time, all 'masters' and so all had studied outside Scotland. The places of study of four of this group are still unknown; but William Fraser, Bishop of St Andrews from 1280 to 1297, probably studied at Oxford; David de Moravia of Moray (1299–1326) at Paris; and Thomas de Dundee of Ross (1296–1321) and Matthew Crambeth of Dunkeld (1288–1309) at Bologna.[12]

At this time, before the Wars of Independence, Scots could of course have gone to England to complete their education, and some certainly did so. The sources are far too scanty for us to tell how many. But in the thirteenth century, the centres of learning in France and Italy were mostly longer established and probably still more distinguished than Oxford and Cambridge. An isolated case of a scholar, probably a Scot, who achieved real eminence at the end of the thirteenth century, was John Duns Scotus, who studied and taught at Cambridge, Oxford and Paris, and died, probably at Cologne, in 1308.[13] His career, studying and teaching both in England and on the Continent, would hardly have been possible for a Scot after the Wars of Independence.

In view of the English connections of Scottish churchmen in the twelfth century, it is not surprising that the architecture of Dunfermline Abbey should show close parallels with Durham Cathedral; and that St Rule's Church in St Andrews, the predecessor of the great cathedral, should be related to the church of Wharram-le-Street in Yorkshire, close to Nostell Priory, from which came Robert, the Bishop of St Andrews who probably directed its building.[14] The design of the choir of Jedburgh, where the triforium arches are contained within

119

the arches of the main piers, has been connected to work at Romsey and Tewkesbury abbeys; while details of the nave capitals are similar to those at Byland in Yorkshire. On the other hand, the plan of Kelso abbey, with its double transepts, west and east, seems to be derived from the Rhineland.[15] There is no narrow provincialism in the church architecture of this time. In the thirteenth century, there are still many parallels with England, notably the plan of Bishop Bondington's rebuilt Cathedral of Glasgow, which closely follows those of Salisbury and Wells.

The church was not the only part of Scottish society to develop close links with England and even with the Continent in the period between the twelfth century and the Wars of Independence. The upper ranks of lay society were also part of a society which straddled not only the Borders between England and Scotland, but also the English Channel. Many held lands in Scotland and England; some like the Balliols in France as well; and though King John's loss of Normandy in 1204 made it difficult to hold on to lands in both England and France, some, for instance the Balliols, managed to do so. John Balliol was eventually able to retreat to what had been the French lands of his family, where he died in 1313.

We can get some impression of the cultural world of these Scottish nobles from those of their buildings which survive; in so far as they themselves had experience of life elsewhere, they drew on that experience in deciding what to build. 'Anglo-Norman' settlers of the twelfth century, for whom defence was probably a significant consideration, often built motte and bailey castles; or earth-work castles which could be constructed relatively easily in suitable spots simply by digging ditches across ridges or promontories. Occasionally, as at Mote of Urr in Kircudbrightshire, the fortifications could be very impressive. We must assume that in most cases, where no tower now survives, there was probably a wooden one on the motte, such as was found at Keir Knowe of Drum in Stirlingshire. Sometimes a stone building or buildings topped the motte, as at the Doune of Invernochty and the Peel of

Lumphanan, both in Aberdeenshire. Parallels for both wooden and stone structures can be found in England: Keir Knowe of Drum is very similar to Abinger Motte in Surrey.[16]

Later, their residences still followed the fashions developing in the south. Stone replaced wood. Curtain walls provided stronger defences, while keeps or 'donjons' in various forms not only afforded security but even comfort. The best-preserved thirteenth-century residence is probably the thirteenth-century tower at Dirleton in East Lothian, a castle of the de Vaux family, who came originally from the neighbourhood of Rouen in Normandy, but different branches settled in Cumberland and East Lothian in the mid-twelfth century. The surviving tower, now part of a structure radically altered in the fourteenth century, gives a remarkable sense of the domestic comfort which a prominent thirteenth century baron would expect. Another tower, probably originally even more impressive, existed in the castle of the *de Moravia* family, at Bothwell in Lanarkshire, but it was partially dismantled in or after 1337 in the later stages of the Wars of Independence. Less complete buildings, which will have had similar facilities, survive at, for example, Rothesay in Bute, Lochindorb in Morayshire and Inverlochy in Inverness-shire. These castles had 'garderobes' and fireplaces, and could reasonably match those to be found in England. At Bothwell, in the late thirteenth century, at Kildrummy in Aberdeenshire and at Carlaverock in Dumfriesshire, there were impressive double gatehouses, reminiscent of the buildings, for instance, at Harlech and Beaumaris in Wales, constructed at the bidding of Edward I. By that time Scottish military architecture was scarcely, if at all, behind the times, though much less has been preserved than of the Edwardian castles in Wales.[17]

We have much less information about the houses of the lower classes. Little indeed is known of the houses of the peasantry or even of lesser rural landowners. They were probably not very different from the basic 'long house' type of surviving rural cottages of much more recent times; or indeed from the 'round houses' of Skara Brae in remote antiquity.

The essentials were dictated by need, not considerations of style. In Scotland the common materials were probably stone and turf, because they were available; rather than wood as in England. At that level, one would hardly expect either foreign contacts or influences.

The other obvious point of contact with England and further afield was in such of the Scottish burghs as had trading connections. We know very little that is precise about Scottish trade before the Wars of Independence, since the earliest customs records only date from 1331,[18] But there is evidence of the existence of some 55 burghs in Scotland before 1296 which possessed trading privileges of a sort.[19] Only a few of these, however, traded significantly outside the kingdom, notably Berwick, and perhaps Perth, Dundee, St Andrews and Aberdeen. Of these, most of our scanty evidence relates to Berwick. For example, in 1213 a ship of Bruges received an English protection to go to Berwick. In 1229, a London merchant, Gervase de Cordwainer, was given an English safe-conduct to ship wool from Berwick; and in 1242 Scottish wool was arrested at Yarmouth in ships of the King of France, with whom Henry III of England was then at war.[20] Such isolated pieces of information can establish no trends, but they make it clear that Scottish trade was significant, even if in these cases it was being carried by foreign merchants.

Foreigners were also commonly settled in Scottish burghs, which often included incomers from Flanders and France as well as from England. An appreciable number of the early burgesses, however, came from eastern English towns, from Orford in Essex to Whitby, Ravenser and York in Yorkshire.[21] On the other hand, Scottish traders certainly had reached the Continent before 1296. Alexander Stevenson points out that there was a Scottish community settled in Bruges by the 1290s: 'Unique among foreign nations, a stretch of the main canal was named after it, the *Schottendyc*, and by that date there was an adjacent street called "Scotland".'[22] We have evidence only of isolated instances of what may well have been a significant involvement of Scottish merchants in the trade of Europe; but it remains likely that the bulk of Scottish trade before 1296 was coastal and with England.

The turning point in Scotland's relations with the rest of Christendom came with the Wars of Independence. However, these did not break all established links. Connections with Ireland, which had been so prominent in earlier centuries, certainly continued. For example, Robert Bruce sent his brother on an expedition in 1315 with the object of making him King of Ireland, a scheme which collapsed with his death at the battle of Dundalk in 1318;[23] and there were political contacts in the fifteenth century. The only survivor of the Albany clan after James I's judicial purge of the family in 1425, James the Fat, took refuge in the Glens of Antrim, where he was protected by a relative of the Lord of the Isles. If we had more knowledge of the history of the Western Highlands and Islands in the fifteenth century, we would probably know more of the connections between Scotland and Ireland in that period. On the other hand, connections with Scandinavia were fading after the settlement of 1266 which ceded the Isles to Scottish control, although Orkney and Shetland remained technically subject to Norway till 1468 and 1469 respectively, when they were pledged to James III as security for the dowry of his Danish bride Margaret, a dowry which was never paid, and hence the islands reverted to Scotland.

But the most dramatic change in Scotland's overseas relations at the end of the thirteenth century was the abrupt rupture of its connections with England; and a consequential strengthening of its connections with mainland Europe.

Once the wars started, trading contacts with England were much reduced, but there is increasing evidence of Scottish trade with the Continent, much of it thereafter by Scottish rather than foreign merchants. Customs records can show that by 1331–3, approximately five-sixths of the total trade was in Scottish hands;[24] but these records do not tell us the destinations of Scottish trade. The best one can do is to observe instances, mainly in foreign records, where we have evidence of individual Scottish merchants, or of Scottish trading communities settled abroad. These are inevitably arbitrary and accidental, and convey no trends; but, to quote David Ditchburn, 'in 1312, St Andrews merchants had their goods seized in Norway'. 'Merchants from Cupar, Dunfermline, Dysart, Haddington, Inverkeithing, Lanark, Peebles and Selkirk were trading with Danzig in 1444.' In 1497, a record of ships passing in and out of the Baltic includes 'twenty-one Scots ships ... seven from Dundee, five from Leith, four each from Aberdeen and St Andrews, and one from an unknown port'.[25]

In the field of higher education, likewise, after 1296, English universities were generally closed to Scots, except for occasional cases where safe-conducts were issued in times of truce. Most Scottish students, at least from the early fourteenth century until the beginnings of St Andrews University in 1411, studied on the Continent; and even thereafter many continued to do so.

A limited number of Scots went on to hold positions as teachers and scholars abroad: John de Rate and Walter Wardlaw in Paris in the 1340s and 1350s; William de Trebrun in the 1380s and Laurence of Lindores in the early years of the fifteenth century, both also at Paris; Scottish doctors taught there in the 1360s and from 1409 to 1416; and Scottish lawyers were teaching at Orléans and Angers for periods in the 1350s and 1370s.[26] Nor did this European link cease when Scotland had its own universities. These perforce had to be staffed at first by men already established with degrees abroad. In the fifteenth century only St Andrews, with the advantage of Laurence of Lindores as one of its first teachers, established anything of a reputation: Glasgow made little mark at first and Aberdeen was only founded at the end of the century, though by 1497 it had attracted the distinguished scholar, Hector Boece, friend of Erasmus and author of the *Scotorum Historiae*, published at Paris in 1526. In 1505, he became the first Principal of the University, a new post established under the constitution of that year. To the end of the middle ages and beyond, Scottish scholars regularly pursued their careers on the Continent. In the early years of the sixteenth century, Paris possessed a distinguished school of 'Scottish nominalists' headed by John Mair, educated first at Cambridge (by the late fifteenth century, English universities were again open to Scots) and then at Paris, where he had a notable career as a teacher of philosophy and theology before returning to Scotland as principal of Glasgow University from 1518 to 1522, then to St Andrews, back to Paris in 1525, and finally returning to St Andrews in 1531 to become Provost of St Salvator's College in 1533.[27]

The number of Scottish students, teachers or pupils, must not be exaggerated. The total remained small – Professor Watt has identified only just over 1000 in the whole period from the twelfth century to 1410, suggesting, as he points out, an average of 'between five and ten young men starting out each year from the whole country'. Even at St Andrews, 'the number of students taking their first degree in the Faculty of Arts ... was to average only ten per year over the first forty years from 1410 to 1450'. The number reaching levels of distinction as scholars was far fewer: to quote Professor Watt, 'only John Duns Scotus and Laurence of Lindores made anything like a lasting name for themselves as scholars as well as teachers'.[28] After the period he was discussing, we should certainly add the names of John Mair and Hector Boece. Yet these graduates, as a body, were the leaders of the Scottish church; and right to the end of the middle ages, they continued to be formed by experiences at the centres of learning of western Europe.

For the aristocracy likewise, the wars severed their links with England: no longer could one talk, if one ever really could, of an 'Anglo-Norman' Scottish nobility. After 1306, it was no longer possible to hold land in both countries, or to be in the allegiance of both kings. The wars themselves, however, opened new opportunities for Scots to go abroad after 1337, when the war between the Kings of England and Scots became a complicated triangular affair involving the French as well.

Since 1295 the kings of Scots were allied to France in a series of treaties which were renewed at intervals during the next two centuries. The threat of French assistance to the Scots had been a factor in Edward III's decision to claim the French crown in 1337, and French forces were in fact sent to Scotland to support the wars against England in 1355 and 1385.

More significantly, the wars in France opened possibilities for Scots to serve in French armies and perhaps win rewards and even lands in France. We hear much of English soldiers of fortune and free companies in France; there were Scots there also, normally and naturally on the French side. There is no full-scale modern study of this interesting subject. The best available collections of material are in two large nineteenth-century works which are not always totally reliable, though very helpful.[29] But there is good evidence that a number of Scots fought on the French side at Poitiers: Fordun's chronicle, composed in the fourteenth century, says that William Lord of Douglas, the future first Earl of Douglas, came 'to give aid to the king of France, bringing with him several from Scotland strong in force, skilled in arms and experienced in war'. Two of the manuscripts give a list of some of those present: William Ramsay and Henry Gray, who were killed; Archibald Douglas ('the Grim' and later third Earl of Douglas) and William Ramsay of Colluthie, who were captured; and William Gladstaines, Robert Livingstone, John Herries and John Grant who were knighted, presumably by the French king before the battle. Also present was Patrick Dunbar, nephew of the then Earl of March and father of George, who succeeded as earl in 1368; Patrick went on crusade after the battle and died while on his journey.[30] In all, this is quite a considerable list of prominent Scots. There were probably many lesser men present as their followers.

Much better known are the activities of the fourth Earl of Douglas, and the Earl of Buchan and a goodly number of followers in the French wars after Agincourt: the Scots troops contributed largely to the defeat and death of the Duke of Clarence at Baugé in 1421; and though both Douglas and

Buchan were killed at Verneuil in 1424, quite a few Scots remained in French service, notably Sir John Stewart of Darnley till his death at the siege of Orléans in 1428. Some remained in France even longer and others arrived after Verneuil, to form the nucleus of the 'Scots Guard' made famous by Sir Walter Scott in *Quentin Durward*.

Some of the Scots received notable rewards: the Earl of Douglas was given the Duchy of Touraine in 1424, a title which remained in his family till the execution of William, the sixth Earl of Douglas, in 1440. Sir John Stewart received the Lordships of Concressault and d'Aubigny, both of which passed to a cadet line which settled in France and became the important family of Stuart d'Aubigny. Thomas Houston was given Gournay by Charles VII, replaced by Torcy en Brie in 1466. Like a number of others, Houston seems to have settled in France and made his career there.[31] Long before the Thirty Years' War, Scots had seen the possibilities of a career in arms wherever opportunity offered. The Hundred Years War provided military opportunities for many of all nationalities; as did the wars in Italy, though any Scots who may have joined in these have so far escaped the attention of scholars.

We can see something more of the foreign contacts of the Scots in the art which they patronised. Much of what survives is, naturally enough, religious art, though much of that suffered in the centuries of neglect that followed the Reformation, as churches fell into ruins or were adapted to very different styles of worship, adaptations in which the ornaments were particularly likely to suffer and liturgical books to disappear. The tomb of Robert Bruce in Dunfermline Abbey, made during the king's lifetime by the Parisian sculptor, Thomas of Chartres, now survives only in fragments in the National Museum in Edinburgh;[32] but there are a conspicuous number of illuminated manuscripts, dating from the fifteenth and early sixteenth centuries, which were produced in the Low Countries and France, evidently for Scottish patrons. Most notable are the Hours of James IV and Margaret Tudor, produced for their wedding in 1503 and described as 'perhaps the finest medieval manuscript to have been commissioned for Scottish use'.[33] It is now in the National Library in Vienna. There is a manuscript of Virgil, produced in France possibly for a daughter of James I; at least three Books of Hours produced in northern France for unidentified Scottish patrons; and a prayerbook, also from northern France, commissioned between 1484 and 1492 for Robert Blackadder, Bishop of Glasgow before he became archbishop in 1492. There are also surviving two much less distinguished academic manuscripts with some illustrations, lectures on logic and a set of commentaries on Aristotle's *Physics*, written in Louvain in the 1460s and 1470s by Scots who were perhaps students there.

Also from France came two of the medieval maces of St Andrews University, and the medieval mace of Glasgow University;[34] this was natural in view of the close connections of the new Scottish universities with French centres of learning, especially Paris. Nor, when we remember Scots trading contacts with the Low Countries, is it any surprise that James III, or perhaps Edward Bonkil, the first provost of Trinity College in Edinburgh, went to Hugo van der Goes for the magnificent altarpiece now in the National Gallery of Scotland, which was painted for the new college around 1478–9. The fine portrait of William Elphinstone, Bishop of Aberdeen from 1488–9 to 1514, and founder of Aberdeen University, possibly once part of a similar altarpiece, also came from the Low Countries,[35] as probably did the impressive carved statue of St Andrew, now in the National Museum in Edinburgh.[36]

Scots were certainly in touch with some of the best centres of medieval art in Northern Europe, especially in northern France and the Low Countries; but this does not mean that native Scottish artists were necessarily inferior. Their best work was perhaps in metalwork and woodcarving, unfortunately forms which are particularly liable to be scattered or to perish with the ravages of time. The Bute Mazer, a maple–wood bowl, with elaborate silver-gilt ornamentation, made in the early fourteenth century, perhaps as a commemoration of the battle of Bannockburn or of the marriage of the Steward to Bruce's daughter Marjorie, is one of the few really notable pieces to have remained in Scottish hands.[37] The Savernake Horn, of which the baldric was certainly, from the heraldic coats of arms represented on it, made for an earl of Moray in the fourteenth century, was perhaps looted by the Earl of Hertford during his invasion of Scotland in 1544. It is now in the British Museum.[38] A fine sixteenth-century lectern is now in the parish church of St Stephens in St Albans, having probably been 'acquired' by Sir Robert Lee of Sopwell during the same invasion.[39] Scottish seal matrixes, too, show very high standards of skill and artistry; as do the surviving late medieval oak panels from Arbroath (the Beaton panels), those from an old house in Montrose which may have come from a hospital founded there by an abbot of Cambuskenneth, and the four carved oak panels from the nunnery at Dundee, now in the National Museum.[40]

There was no conflict between wide international contacts and the developing sense of national identity which we have traced in previous chapters. Fifteenth-century churchmen were perhaps more involved than any other class in the wider world: since they were part of a universal institution, their profession demanded such involvement. Yet the result was the development of what can only be called liturgical nationalism. For centuries, the Scots had had to rely on service books of foreign origin, principally based on the English 'Use of Sarum', the calendars of which inevitably emphasised English saints, alongside those whose cults were universal. Scotland had no lack of saints; but their services had to be included in the liturgy by local initiative in individual dioceses. When Scottish clergy, such as Bishop Elphinstone of Aberdeen, travelled abroad on their business, they found that liturgical reform was in the air; and the result, in Scotland as in other places such as Norway, was a realisation of the need for a *Scottish* liturgy which would give a proper place to Scottish saints in the calendar. Elphinstone set about organising the preparation of such a national breviary by his cathedral clergy and others with whom he had contacts, a breviary from which many lesser English saints were removed and others liturgically downgraded, to make room for Scottish saints. This move clearly had a political as well as a religious motive and it was strongly supported by King James IV. His patent to the printers Chepman & Myllar in 1507 explicitly included the printing of a Scottish service book, and ordered that 'na maner of sic bukis of Salusbery use be brocht to be sauld within our realm in tym cuming'. The result was the *Aberdeen Breviary*, duly printed in 1510. It is now a very rare book, not only because the Reformation caused widespread destruction of all 'popish' service books, but also because it was before long overtaken by the thorough revision of the Roman breviary at the bidding of Popes Clement VII and Pius V. Nevertheless, the *Aberdeen Breviary* demonstrated that the universalism of the medieval church was no barrier to the maintenance of a national identity.[41]

The same blending of foreign influences and concern for Scottish identity has recently been observed in the architecture of late medieval Scotland.[42] A number of important churches were rebuilt or extended in the fifteenth century, in styles clearly derived from early medieval Romanesque. Fifteenth-century work at Melrose Abbey, Dunkeld Cathedral, St Machar's Cathedral at Aberdeen and at lesser churches such as St Mary's, Haddington and the Church of the Holy Rude at Stirling, all include round arches or drum pillars in Romanesque style. Yet Melrose, for instance, also has window traceries and flying buttresses which were clearly French in inspiration. Royal works show similar mixing of older Scottish and continental styles. Linlithgow palace has both round-headed windows and round arches, combined with many details and an overall plan which follow contemporary Italian models. It may be that the Romanesque elements in fifteenth-century Scottish architecture were a deliberate return to the traditions of Scotland's 'golden age' in the early days of the Canmore dynasty. They are, it is suggested, a conscious proclamation of a Scottish identity, to be set beside the work of the national historians already discussed in Chapter 5.

Scotland in the middle ages was no isolated backwater. She was in touch with a wide range of societies from Ireland and Scandinavia to France, the Low Countries and northern Germany. Her merchants were familiar in ports around the North Sea and the Baltic, from Bruges to Danzig; churchmen from Scotland were frequent visitors on business at the papal court, and even more frequent petitioners there; and Scots were familiar with the culture and learning of western Europe. None of this weakened the strong sense of a national identity which had been formed in the years of peace under the Canmore dynasty and strengthened during the two centuries of intermittent conflict with England which followed the tragedy of 1286. This sense of a national identity was to remain important in the complex conflicts and cross-currents of the age of the Reformation, and for long after.

EPILOGUE: A NEW AGE?

The disaster at Flodden in 1513, when James IV's entry into the war against Henry VIII resulted in his own death and that of most of his leading nobles, left Scotland yet again in a highly problematic minority. The new king, born only the year before, was not to exercise royal authority in person, even formally, till 1526, when he reached the age of fourteen. James IV had left an ambiguous legacy for those who had to decide the orientation of Scottish policy in the increasingly turbulent and convoluted politics of the sixteenth century. His marriage to Margaret Tudor left a Queen Dowager anxious to assert her authority and naturally inclined towards an alliance with her brother Henry VIII of England. But the heir presumptive to the infant King was John Duke of Albany, who had been brought up in France following his father's exile in 1483, after an ultimately abortive rising in 1482 against James III;[1] and when he was recognised as 'Lord Governor of Scotland' in 1515, he was equally naturally inclined to turn Scottish policy towards France.

In the event, the politics of the minority proved far more complex than these simple polarities might suggest; but the issue of peace or war with England was to divide Scottish policy at least until 1560. Moreover, as Jenny Wormald has convincingly argued, the ending of the Hundred Years' War in 1453, and with that the ending of the period of more or less continuous Anglo-Scottish warfare which had accompanied it, led to a much more marked attempt by Scots to assert themselves on a European stage and to develop contacts, particularly artistic and cultural, with the centres and central figures of the European renaissance.[2] As we have seen, Scottish scholars were a distinctive group at the intellectual centre at Paris; Erasmus, one of the leading figures in the intellectual life of Europe at the time, not only acted as a tutor to James IV's apparently very able illegitimate son, Alexander Stewart, Archbishop of St Andrews from 1504 (when he was aged about 11!) till his death at Flodden, but also was in contact with other Scots, notably Hector Boece, the Principal of Aberdeen University. Such European contacts were not unprecedented, but the scale and range of Scottish involvement in Europe certainly extended greatly in the early sixteenth century; something which the Reformation was to increase even more dramatically.

What effect were these developments to have on the sense of a Scottish identity, which had for so long expressed itself in hostility to England?

The peace with England which followed Flodden was by no means complete. In 1523, Albany could still lead a Franco-Scottish army to fight the English at Wark, though the Scottish troops showed little anxiety to join the battle. In the 1540s, the Earl of Hertford, later Duke of Somerset, led three invasions of Scotland. Anglo-Scottish wars were not over; and on the Borders raiding continued, despite efforts by the governments on both sides to check it; and ballads, such as 'Johnie Armstrang' and 'Kinmont Willie', mostly dating from these or later times, show that the ideals of maintaining a Scottish identity and independence against the English were not forgotten.

But there were those, like the scholar John Mair, who had studied at Cambridge before going to Paris, who argued that peace was better than war and unity than division; and many Scots agreed. There were Scottish nobles in English pay in Henry VIII's time, who were not necessarily simply bought time-servers. In the 1540s, James Henrisoun, a burgess of Edinburgh who had migrated to England with Hertford's retreating army in 1544, produced at least two pieces of propaganda arguing for the union of Scotland and England,[3] a union which by then seemed particularly attractive to those who hoped that Scotland would soon follow England in establishing a church independent of Rome.

Indeed, the progress of the Reformation might easily seem to make the defence of a particular Scottish identity irrelevant. Knox and many of his colleagues were preachers of a universal Protestantism, whether it took shape in Geneva, Frankfurt, England or Scotland. What mattered was not national independence, but the destruction of Antichrist, in the person of the Pope; and to that end, Elizabeth, or even more James VI, ultimately to become James VI and I, might appear as the great defender of the true church on a universal stage. At this point, the defence of a Scottish identity might easily fade away.

But the progress of the Reformation was not so simple. There were many who did not share Knox's apocalyptic vision, which drew heavily on the pages of Revelation. Other influential Scottish Protestants were more inclined to maintain the spiritual integrity of Scotland and less interested in the last things of Revelation. Elizabeth herself was markedly reluctant to take on the part of universal saviour of the true church. James, who did have universal aspirations, was by no means committed to the purity of the Scottish church, being more than a little attracted to an erastian episcopalianism which suited ill with the notions of independence and 'democracy' of the Kirk. Hence rifts opened between Scottish and English Protestants, in which, especially after 1603, James's ideals might easily seem a revival in different form of the 'British' imperialism of Edward I.[4]

In that situation a very different strand emerged, which drew upon the ideals of the historical nationalism of Fordun and Bower, elaborated as it had been in the writing of Hector Boece, the friend of Erasmus and a firm Catholic. Boece's History, published in 1526,[5] developed the early history of the Scots, drawing, he claimed, on the writings of a thirteenth-century canon of Aberdeen called Veremund,[6] from which he was able to give details of the careers of all the kings of Scots between Fergus I and Fergus II. Boece became in the sixteenth century the most widely read propagator of the myths asserting the ancient and unchallenged independence of the Scottish nation. These stories were taken over by the leading Protestant humanist and historian, George Buchanan, who, arguing in support of the deposition of Mary Queen of Scots, developed them as evidence of the long-standing right of the Scottish nobles, speaking for the people, to reject and overthrow errant rulers, a process of which Boece's and Buchanan's accounts of the early kings provided numerous examples.[7] John Mair, in his *History of Greater Britain*, had developed a contract theory of the basis of government long before Hobbes, Locke and Rousseau made such ideas common; and these ideas were taken up by Buchanan and others at the time to bolster their doctrines of the right of revolution. The young James VI, whose tutor Buchanan for a time was, was naturally unimpressed by these theories.[8]

For all these reasons, the progress of the Reformation and the development of Reformation politics had thrown up many conflicts between Scots and English to disturb the ideal of a united Protestant British realm which had seemed so attractive to Henrisoun and Knox. The debates over a possible 'union' in the first years of James VI and I as King of England, and the subsequent policies of both James and Charles, created many more. In the end, the notion of a Scottish identity was to be reinforced, not overtaken by the developments of the sixteenth and seventeenth centuries; and the persecution of the Covenanters in the 'killing time' of the 1680s was to be added to all the myths of Scottish identity which were inherited from the middle ages. Some parts of these myths were already fading. The early kings and their doings were being trenchantly attacked by the 'British' party in the sixteenth century, notably the Welshman Humphrey Lluyd, who plagued Buchanan by denouncing only too effectively Boece's account of these kings. Buchanan's own use of the early legends to argue for a peculiarly Scottish 'ancient constitution' was to be demolished by Jacobites in the eighteenth century, especially by Father Thomas Innes in his brilliant *Critical Essay on the Ancient Inhabitants of the Northern Parts of Britain or Scotland* (first published in London in 1729). But other parts of the medieval case remained: the resistance to the English, the Wars of Independence, Wallace, Bruce, the Declaration of Arbroath, and the Border Ballads, were still arguments in good fettle ready to be used by the defenders of a Scottish identity in the seventeenth century and in the debates about the Union, which was reluctantly accepted by the Scottish Parliament in 1707. They were there to be drawn on by Burns and Scott as they developed their ideas of a Scottish identity in the very changed times of the late eighteenth and early nineteenth centuries.

The essential identity of Scotland consists not in culture or language. It depends on a sense that Scotland, many-sided as it may be, is a country that came together in the middle ages and established itself in a long struggle against the threats of absorption by its more powerful and wealthy southern neighbour; a country that emerged from this time of troubles strengthened and with a continuing sense of identity which subsumed all its internal variations and disputes; an identity which remains hard to define but which can be clearly perceived and which does not depend on political inde-pendence or self-government. The sense of identity is as clear today after almost three centuries of union as it was in the middle ages or the age of the Reformation.

It is by no means the only such distinct identity which exists within the 'states' of Europe in the late twentieth century. It may remind us that the maintenance of the identity in a nation may be as important as the preservation of a sense of identity in a person. Both can at times be destructive, for one way of establishing both kinds of identity is to attack others; but it is not the only way. After the Act of Union, Scots in the eighteenth and nineteenth centuries contributed a great deal to Britain and the Empire, to the industrial revolution through their inventions, to medicine, to science, to administration and government at home and in the Empire. From Lord Roseberry to Sir Alec Douglas Hume, five or six Scots, depending on whether one counts Bonar Law as Scot or Canadian, have been Prime Ministers of Great Britain. None of these inventors, doctors, scientists, colonial administrators or politicians lost the sense that they were Scottish, as well as British. The two identities could co-exist without difficulty. What is disastrous is the attempt to destroy identities, not the existence of identities which can overlap without conflict, indeed often with great profit. From that point of view, the Scottish experience may offer important lessons well outside its own borders.

NOTES AND REFERENCES

INTRODUCTION: THE PROBLEM OF A SCOTTISH IDENTITY

1. *The New Testament in Scots*, trans. W. L. Lorimer (1983); rev. edn (London, 1985). There were a number of earlier translations, one by Murdoch Nisbet produced around 1520, but not printed till 1901–5, and several in the nineteenth and twentieth centuries. For details, see Graham Tulloch, *A History of the Scots Bible* (Aberdeen, 1989).
2. Marinell Ash, *The Strange Death of Scottish History* (Edinburgh, 1980), p. 151.

1 THE IDENTITY OF PLACE

1. *The Anglo-Saxon Chronicle*, trans. G. N. Garmonsway (London & New York, 1953), p. 82 (AD 891). The Anglo-Saxon text reads *Scottas.*
2. Graham and Anna Ritchie, *Scotland: Archaeology and Early History* (Edinburgh, 1991), pp. 89–94.
3. Ibid., p. 124.
4. Ibid., pp. 149–50.
5. A. P. Smyth, *Warlords and Holy Men* (London, 1984), pp. 43–5.
6. *Venerabilis Baedae Historiam Ecclesiasticam Gentis Anglorum*, ed. C. Plummer (Oxford, 1896), I, p. 133 (Bk 3, ch. 4); but see A. A. M. Duncan, *Scotland: The Making of the Kingdom* (Edinburgh, 1975), pp. 46, 69–70.
7. Smyth, *Warlords and Holy Men*, p. 63
8. I have drawn here on ideas put forward by Dr Dauvit Broun in a paper on 'Defining Scotland before the Wars of Independence', given at the 1994 conference of the Association of Scottish

Historical Studies, of which a text was included in the circulated conference papers.

9. *Regesta Regum Scottorum*, II, ed. G. W. S. Barrow with W. W. Scott (Edinburgh, 1971), no. 61.

10. *Regesta Regum Scottorum*, V, ed. A. A. M. Duncan (Edinburgh, 1988), p. 54, and the examples given there.

11. K. A. Steer and J. W. M. Bannerman, *Late Medieval Monumental Sculpture in the West Highlands* (HMSO, 1977), pp. 180–4.

12. John G. Dunbar, *The Historic Architecture of Scotland* (London, 1966), pp. 24–5.

13. Harold W. Booton, 'Inland trade: a study of Aberdeen in the later middle ages,' in *The Scottish Medieval Town*, ed. Michael Lynch, Michael Spearman and Geoffrey Stell (Edinburgh, 1988), p. 155.

14. *The Bruce, by John Barbour*, ed. W. M. Mackenzie (London, 1909), p. 159 (Bk 9, line 403).

2 THE IDENTITY OF ORDER

1. Duncan, *Scotland*, pp. 93–5.

2. Barbara E. Crawford, *Scandinavian Scotland* (Leicester, 1987), pp. 53–6.

3. Duncan, *Scotland*, pp. 110–11.

4. Ibid., Genealogical Tree 1.

5. Crawford, *Scandinavian Scotland*, pp. 74, 77; G. W. S. Barrow, *Kingship and Unity: Scotland 1000–1306* (London, 1981), p. 27; Duncan, *Scotland*, pp. 100, 118.

6. F. L. Ganshof, *La Flandre sous les Premiers Comtes* (Brussels, 1949), ch. 6, especially pp. 104–6.

7. *The Anglo-Saxon Chronicle*, trans. Garmonsway, p. 208.

8. Ibid., p. 228.

9. Ibid.

10. Ibid., p. 230

11. G. W. S. Barrow, *The Anglo-Norman Era in Scottish History* (Oxford, 1980), pp. 61–4.

12. 'The earliest Stewarts and their lands' in G. W. S. Barrow, *The Kingdom of the Scots* (London, 1973), pp. 337–61, especially pp. 355–61.

13. Barrow, *The Anglo-Norman Era*, p. 50.

14. *The Sheriff Court Book of Fife, 1515–1522*, ed. W. Croft Dickinson (Scottish History Society, 3rd series, vol. 12, 1928), pp. 349–55.
15. Ibid., pp. xi–xiii.
16. 'The justiciar', in Barrow, *The Kingdom of the Scots*, pp. 83–138.
17. For the text see *English Historical Documents ii, 1042–1189*, ed. D. C. Douglas and G. W. Greenaway (London, 1953), p. 475.
18. *The Register of Brieves*, ed. Lord Cooper (Stair Society, vol. 10, 1946), pp. 40–1.
19. I am grateful to Dr A. L. Murray for very helpful comments on this point.
20. *Regesta Regum Scottorum*, VI, ed. Bruce Webster (Edinburgh, 1982), p. 12.
21. *Regesta Regum Scottorum*, V, pp. 174–7, scribes H, L, M, and a number of 'unique hands'; *Regesta Regum Scottorum*, VI, pp. 12–13, scribes viii, xiv, xvi, xviii, xxiii, xxv, xxxii and xlvii.
22. Bruce Webster, *Scotland from the Eleventh Century to 1603* (Sources of History, 1975), pp. 122–7.
23. Barrow, *Kingship and Unity*, pp. 84–104.
24. G. S. Pryde, *The Burghs of Scotland* (London, 1965), pp. 3–8.
25. *Regesta Regum Scottorum*, II, map at end.
26. *Anglo-Saxon Chronicle*, trans. Garmonsway, p. 213, Ms D, 1078; A. O. Anderson, *Early Sources of Scottish History AD 500 to 1286* (Edinburgh & London, 1922), II, p. 46.
27. Duncan, *Scotland*, pp. 165–7.
28. Anderson, *Early Sources*, II, pp. 173–4.
29. Duncan, *Scotland*, pp. 138–9.
30. Pryde, *Burghs of Scotland*, nos 8, 13.
31. Anderson, *Early Sources*, II, p. 251. Anderson translates *transtulit* in the Latin text as 'transported'.
32. Duncan, *Scotland*, pp. 191–8.
33. A. A. M. Duncan and A. L. Brown, 'Argyll and the Isles in the earlier middle ages', *Proceedings of the Society of Antiquaries of Scotland*, vol. 90 (1956–7), pp. 195–9.
34. Anderson, *Early Sources*, II, pp. 244–5.
35. Duncan, *Scotland*, pp. 181–4.
36. Ibid., p. 186.
37. Grant G. Simpson and Bruce Webster, 'Charter evidence and the distribution of mottes in Scotland', *Essays on the Nobility of Medieval Scotland*, ed. K. J. Stringer (Edinburgh, 1985), pp. 9–10.
38. See above, notes 8–10.

39. A. O. Anderson, *Early Sources*, II, p. 244.

40. A. O. Anderson, *Scottish Annals from English Chroniclers, AD 500 to 1286* (London, 1908), p. 330, n. 6.

41. H. Pierquin, *Receuil Général des Chartes Anglo-Saxonnes* (Paris, 1912), pp. 476, 479. The significance of these titles is discussed in E. John, *Orbis Britanniae* (Leicester, 1966), pp. 52–9.

42. *Anglo-Scottish Relations, 1174–1328: Some Selected Documents*, ed. E. L. G. Stones (London & Edinburgh, 1965), p. 1.

43. Ibid., pp. 6–7; see also Duncan, *Scotland*, pp. 236–8.

44. D. E. R. Watt, 'The minority of Alexander III of Scotland', *Transactions of the Royal Historical Society* (5th series), 21 (1971), pp. 2–6.

45. *Johannis de Fordun Chronica Gentis Scotorum*, ed. W. F. Skene (*The Historians of Scotland*, I, Edinburgh, 1871), p. 293; *Scotichronicon by Walter Bower*, ed. D. E. R. Watt and others (Aberdeen 1987–), V, pp. 290–3.

46. *Fordun*, ed. Skene, I, pp. 294–5; *Scotichronicon*, ed. Watt, V, pp. 292–5.

47. *Scotichronicon*, ed. Watt., V, 441, citing M. O. Anderson, *Kings and Kingship in Early Scotland* (Edinburgh & London, 1980), pp. 214, 238, 256–7, 293.

48. The most recent detailed discussion is in John Bannerman, 'The king's poet and the inauguration of Alexander III', *Scottish Historical Review*, 68(1989), pp. 120–49.

49. Ailred of Rievaulx, '*Epistola ad illustrem ducem H[enricum]*' in R. Twysden, *Historiae Anglicanae Scriptores Decem* (London, 1652), I, column 348: 'obsequia illa quae a gente Scottorum in novella regum promotione more patrio exhibentur ita exhorruit, ut ea vix ab episcopis suscipere cogeretur'.

50. Cf., for instance, the inauguration ceremonies of Edward IV and Richard III of England which preceded their 'coronations', in the first case by more than three months, in the second by ten days. See C. A. J. Armstrong, 'The inauguration ceremonies of the Yorkist kings and their title to the throne', *Transactions of the Royal Historical Society* (4th series), 30 (1948), pp. 51–73. Both reigns were dated from the inauguration, not the coronation. The normal English practice was, and is, to date reigns from the death of the previous monarch, with the coronation following when convenient. These two are significant because, not being normal accessions by the next heir, they reveal ideas on the significance of inaugurations and coronations.

51. *Scotichronicon*, ed. Watt., V, pp. 196–9, 442, citing *Dunfermline Registrum*, no. 348 for the attendance.
52. For example, ibid., pp. 420–9.

3 THE IDENTITY OF FAITH

1. Michael Lynch, *Scotland: A New History* (London, 1991), pp. 28–36.
2. Smyth, *Warlords and Holy Men*, pp. 102–7.
3. Duncan, *Scotland*, p. 71.
4. *Adomnan's Life of Columba*, ed. A. O. and M. O. Anderson (Edinburgh, 1961).
5. Smyth, *Warlords and Holy Men*, pp. 65–6.
6. Ibid., pp. 185–8; Anderson, *Early Sources*, I, pp. 259–61, 263–6.
7. Anderson, *Early Sources*, p. 279 and n. 4; Smyth, *Warlords and Holy Men*, pp. 187–8.
8. Anderson, *Early Sources*, p. 296.
9. *Bede Ecclesiastical History*, ed. Plummer, I, p. 333 (Bk 5, ch. 21); translated in Anderson, *Scottish Annals*, p. 48.
10. Duncan, *Scotland*, p. 71.
11. Smyth, *Warlords and Holy Men*, pp. 186–7.
12. *Chronicles of the Picts, Chronicles of the Scots, and other Early Memorials of Scottish History*, ed. W. F. Skene (Edinburgh, 1867), pp. 138–40, 183–8, 375–7. See also Ursula Hall, *St Andrew and Scotland* (St Andrews, 1994), pp. 60–77.
13. Smyth, *Warlords and Holy Men*, pp. 228–9.
14. The text is printed in *Facsimiles of English Royal Writs to A.D. 1100*, ed. T. A. M. Bishop and P. Chaplais (Oxford, 1957), at plate xxix.
15. *Bede Ecclesiastical History*, ed. Plummer, I, 63–4 (Bk 1, ch. 29).
16. *Anglo-Saxon Chronicle*, trans. Garmonsway, p. 201.
17. Ibid.
18. Translated in Anderson, *Early Sources*, II, 59–88.
19. Ibid., II, 31–2.
20. There is no convenient edition. A translation of most of the text is to be found scattered through Anderson, *Early Sources*; for the original, one has to use either the very old text in the Bannatyne Club edition, *Chronica de Mailros* (1835) or, if one can read it, the facsimile edition, *The Chronicle of Melrose*, ed. A. O. Anderson and others (London, 1936).

21. A. Fliche, *La Réforme Grégorienne* (Paris, 1924–37; reprinted 1978), II, p. 280.

22. See examples in *The Letters of John of Salisbury*, I, ed. W. J. Millor, H. E. Butler and C. N. L. Brooke (Edinburgh, 1955), nos 2, 4, 62, 63, 65, 66, 68, etc.

23. Anderson, *Scottish Annals*, pp. 97–8.

24. Ibid., pp. 129–32; see also M. Brett, *The English Church under Henry I* (Oxford, 1975), pp. 17–18.

25. A. W. Haddan and W. Stubbs, *Councils and Ecclesiastical Documents relating to Great Britain and Ireland*, II, part 1 (Oxford, 1873), pp. 202–4.

26. Ibid., pp. 200–2, and *Eadmer's Historia Novorum in Anglia* (Rolls Series, no. 81, 1884), ed. M. Rule, pp. 279–88.

27. R. Somerville, *Scotia Pontificia* (Oxford, 1982), nos 34, 40.

28. Ibid., no 11. For what can be worked out about this episode, see M. Brett, *The English Church*, pp. 22–5. It seems from this account that Henry I was again, as in the case of Turgot, inclined to support Scottish resistance to York.

29. Somerville, *Scotia Pontificia*, no. 40, 13 March, 1157–9.

30. Anderson, *Early Sources*, II, p. 49.

31. Somerville, *Scotia Pontificia*, no. 3.

32. Ibid., no. 34.

33. Ibid., no. 46.

34. Ibid., no. 68.

35. Ibid., nos 47–53.

36. R. Somerville, *Pope Alexander III and the Council of Tours* (Publications of the Centre for Medieval and Renaissance Studies of the University of California, Los Angeles, no. 12, Berkeley, 1977), p. 29.

37. R. Somerville, *Scotia Pontificia*, no. 54; text in full in *Registrum Episcopatus Glasguensis* (Bannatyne and Maitland Clubs, 1843), I, no. 19.

38. Somerville, *Scotia Pontificia*, no. 57*.

39. *Anglo-Scottish Relations*, ed. Stones, pp. 1–2.

40. Somerville, *Scotia Pontificia*, no. 69.

41. Ibid., no. 76.

42. Ibid., no. 80.

43. Ibid., no. 156. See now also A. D. M. Barrell, 'The background to *Cum Universi*: Scoto-papal relations, 1159–1192,' *Innes Review*, 46 (1995), pp. 116–38.

44. *British Library Harleian Manuscript 433*, ed. R. Horrox and P. W. Hammond (Richard III Society, 1979–83), III, pp. 76–98.
45. D. E. R. Watt, 'The Provincial Council of the Scottish church, 1215–1472', in *Medieval Scotland, Crown, Lordship and Community*, ed. A. Grant and K. J. Stringer (Edinburgh, 1993), pp. 140–55.
46. *Fordun*, ed. Skene, pp. 259, 280, 294–5.
47. Hall, *St Andrew and Scotland*, pp. 107–9.

4 THE WARS OF INDEPENDENCE

1. *Anglo-Scottish Relations*, ed. Stones, pp. 38–41.
2. Translated in part in *A Source Book of Scottish History*, ed. W. C. Dickinson, G. Donaldson, and I. A. Milne (Edinburgh, 1952), I, pp. 107–9. Note now the very interesting suggestion that it may have been the Scots and/or King Eric of Norway who first proposed the marriage. See G. W. S. Barrow, 'A kingdom in crisis: Scotland and the Maid of Norway', *Scottish Historical Review*, 69 (1990), pp. 127, 130–1.
3. *Source Book of Scottish History*, I, pp. 105–6.
4. G. W. S. Barrow, *Robert Bruce and the Community of the Realm of Scotland* (3rd edn, Edinburgh, 1988), p. 29.
5. *Source Book of Scottish History*, I, pp. 105–6.
6. Barrow, *Bruce*, pp. 15–16.
7. Ibid., 17–18.
8. *Edward I and the Throne of Scotland, 1290–1296*, ed. E. L. G. Stones and Grant G. Simpson (Oxford, 1978), II, pp. 3–4.
9. Ibid., I, pp. 8, 102–3.
10. Ibid., II, pp. 16–19.
11. The surviving documents in the case are printed in full and discussed in Stones and Simpson, *Edward I*, I (Introduction) and II (Texts).
12. Ibid., II, p. 33.
13. Ibid., II, p. 31.
14. Barrow, *Bruce*, pp. 51–2, 57–9, 62–3.
15. A. A. M. Duncan, 'The early parliaments of Scotland', *Scottish Historical Review*, 45 (1966), pp. 37–47.
16. Barrow, *Bruce*, pp. 63–5.
17. Ibid., pp. 69–74.
18. *Anglo-Scottish Relations*, ed. Stones, no. 27; for Balliol's transfer to France, see Barrow, *Bruce*, p. 95.

19. Barrow, *Bruce*, pp. 83–9.
20. Ibid., pp. 145–52
21. Ibid., ch. 14; and A. A. M. Duncan, 'The war of the Scots, 1306–1323', *Transactions of the Royal Historical Society* (6th series), 2 (1992), pp. 125–51.
22. Ranald Nicholson, *Scotland: The Later Middle Ages* (Edinburgh, 1974; paperback edn, 1978), pp. 119–20.
23. Bruce Webster, 'Scotland without a king, 1329–1341', *Crown, Lordship and Community*, ed. Grant and Stringer, pp. 223–38.
24. A. A. M. Duncan, '*Honi soit qui mal y pense*: David II and Edward III, 1346–52', *Scottish Historical Review*, 67 (1988), pp. 113–14, 121–4.
25. *Anglo-Scottish Relations*, ed. Stones, pp. xxviii–ix, 81–7.
26. T. Rymer, *Foedera, etc.* (Record Commission, 1816–69), I, part 2, pp. 926–7.
27. *Anglo-Scottish Relations*, ed. Stones, p. 97.
28. *Scotichronicon*, ed. Watt, VI, pp. 182–3.
29. Ibid., pp. 134–89.
30. Barrow, *Bruce*, p. 119; see, however, R. G. Goldstein, 'The Scottish mission to Boniface VIII in 1301: a reconsideration of the context of the *Instructiones* and *Processus*', *Scottish Historical Review*, 70 (1991), pp. 1–15.
31. Translated in *A Source Book of Scottish History*, ed. Dickinson, Donaldson and Milne, I, p. 125; for the correct date, however, see Barrow, *Bruce*, pp. 184–5.
32. Quoted from the translation in A. A. M. Duncan, *The Nation of Scots and the Declaration of Arbroath* (Historical Association, London, 1970), pp. 34–7.
33. Thomas I. Rae, *The Administration of the Scottish Frontier, 1513–1603* (Edinburgh, 1966), pp. 170, 261–3.
34. 'Johnie Armstrang' (Child, no. 169) in *The Poetical Works of Sir Walter Scott, Bart.*, vol. 1 (Edinburgh, 1833), pp. 411, 413.
35. See the map at the end of *Regesta Regum Scottorum*, II, showing places of issue of the acts of William I.
36. *Fordun*, ed. Skene, I, 365–7; and *Androw of Wyntoun's Orygynale Cronykil of Scotland*, ed. D. Laing (Edinburgh, 1872) II, 469–70.
37. Barrow, *Bruce*, pp. 293–4; *Regesta Regum Scottorum*, V, no. 301.
38. Contrast, for instance, the map at the end of *Regesta Regum Scottorum*, VI, showing the places of issue of the acts of David II with the map of the acts of William I, cited in note 35 above.

5 THE NATIONAL IDENTITY

1. The acts issued during David's captivity are printed in *Regesta Regum Scottorum*, VI, pp. 139–73; only nos 112, 133, 137, 138, 141, 143 and 146 were issued by the Steward as Lieutenant.
2. *The Exchequer Rolls of Scotland*, ed. J. Stuart and G. Burnett (Edinburgh, 1878) I, pp. 545–93. The only sheriff's account to survive which was rendered during David's captivity is printed ibid., pp. 542–4.
3. Of the 520 acts recorded in *Regesta Regum Scottorum*, VI, 344 were issued after David's return in 1357; to this must be added a further 234 recorded only in the Register of the Great Seal. This record only exists in full from the 1360s; earlier rolls are lost though some record of their contents remains, see *Registrum Magni Sigilli Regum Scotorum*, I, ed. J. M. Thomson (Edinburgh, 1912), appendices 1 and 2.
4. Bruce Webster, 'David II and the government of fourteenth-century Scotland', *Transactions of the Royal Historical Society* (5th series), 16 (1966), pp. 120–1.
5. Nicholson, *Scotland: The Later Middle Ages*, pp. 169–70.
6. Ibid., pp. 178–9.
7. Ibid., pp. 179–80, 182–3.
8. Duncan, 'David II and Edward III', *Scottish Historical Review*, 67 (1988), pp. 113–38.
9. A. Grant, 'The Otterburn War from the Scottish point of view', *War and Border Societies in the Middle Ages*, ed. A. Goodman and A. Tuck (London & New York, 1992), pp. 40–3.
10. Nicholson, *Scotland: The Later Middle Ages*, pp. 189–90, 199–201.
11. Stephen Boardman, 'The man who would be king: the lieutenancy and death of David, duke of Rothesay, 1399–1402', in *People and Power in Scotland*, ed. Roger Mason and Norman Macdougall (Edinburgh, 1992), pp. 1–27.
12. Nicholson, *Scotland: The Later Middle Ages*, ch. 9.
13. For the 'national literature', see F. Brie, *Die Nationale Literatur Schottlands von den Anfängen bis zur Renaissans* (Halle, 1937).
14. *The Bruce by John Barbour*, ed. W. M. Mackenzie (London, 1909), p. xvii.
15. *Johannis de Fordun Chronica Gentis Scotorum*, ed. W. F. Skene (*The Historians of Scotland*, I, Edinburgh, 1871), pp. xiv and xlix–li, where there is printed the preface included in two of the MSS of an abbreviated version of Bower's extension of Fordun's original work.

16. Fordun's sources for his early history are discussed in detail in the introductions by J. and W. MacQueen to vols I and II of *Scotichronicon*, ed. Watt.
17. *Fordun*, ed. Skene, I, pp. 46–9.
18. See *Androw of Wyntoun's Orygynale Cronykil of Scotland*, ed. David Laing (3 vols) (*The Historians of Scotland*, II, III and IX, Edinburgh, 1872–79). There is a later edition published by the Scottish Text Society (1903–14).
19. *Wyntoun*, ed. Laing, III, p. xi.
20. Ibid., p. 101.
21. *Wyntoun*, ed. Laing, II, pp. 302–5.
22. Michael Brown, *James I* (Edinburgh, 1994), ch. 2.
23. Ibid., ch. 4.
24. Nicholson, *Scotland: The Later Middle Ages*, pp. 293–9. Henry V's admonition to the Benedictines is discussed in David Knowles, *The Religious Orders in England*, II (Cambridge, 1955; reprinted 1979), pp. 182–3; James I's letter is in *Scotichronicon*, ed. Watt, VIII, pp. 316–9.
25. Michael Brown, 'That old Serpent and Ancient of Evil Days', *Scottish Historical Review*, 71 (1992), pp. 23–45; and *James I*, ch. 8.
26. Christine McGladdery, *James II* (Edinburgh, 1990), pp. 23–4.
27. Ibid., pp. 57–8, 70.
28. Ibid., pp. 62–70.
29. Ibid., ch. 5.
30. The only full text is still the eighteenth-century edition under the title *Joannis de Fordun Scotichronicon cum supplementis et continuatione Walteri Boweri*, ed. Walter Goodall (2 vols, Edinburgh, 1759). A modern edition, planned in nine volumes, under the general editorship of D. E. R. Watt, is in progress. Seven volumes have appeared, under the title *Scotichronicon by Walter Bower* (Aberdeen and subsequently Edinburgh, 1987–).
31. *Scotichronicon*, ed. Watt, VIII, 340–1. The Latin text is a doggerel couplet: *Non Scotus est Christe / cui liber non placet iste.*
32. Ibid., pp. 302–41.
33. For the whole reign, see Norman Macdougall, *James III: A Political Study* (Edinburgh, 1982). The conflicts between Mary of Gueldres and Bishop Kennedy, and their respective achievements, are discussed on pp. 51–65.
34. *Vita Nobilissimi Defensoris Scotie Willelmi Wallace Militis*, ed. M. P. McDiarmid (Scottish Text Society, 4th series, 1968–9).
35. Norman Macdougall, *James IV* (Edinburgh, 1989).

36. Ibid., pp. 251–61. The quotation is on p. 251.
37. Ibid., p. 254.
38. 'Epistola abbatis Rievallensis Ailredi ad illustrem ducem H. set postmodum Anglorum regem', in *Historiae Anglicanae Scriptores X*, ed. R. Twysden (London, 1652), I, column 348.
39. *Scotichronicon*, ed. Goodall, II, 361.
40. But see A. A. M. Duncan, *James I, 1424–1437* (University of Glasgow, Scottish History Department Occasional Papers, 1976), pp. 13–15.

6 SCOTLAND AND CHRISTENDOM

1. Quoted from the translation in Duncan, *Nation of Scots*, p. 36.
2. *Tacitus on Britain and Germany*, trans. H. Mattingly (Penguin Books, 1948), p. 60.
3. Smyth, *Warlords and Holy Men*, p. 16.
4. Graham and Anna Ritchie, *Scotland: Archaeology and Early History*, pp. 149–51, 160–9.
5. J. B. Stevenson, *Exploring Scotland's Heritage: The Clyde Estuary and Central Region* (Edinburgh, 1985), pp. 106–7.
6. *The Anglo-Saxon Chronicle*, trans. Garmonsway, p. 82.
7. Anderson, *Early Sources*, I, p. 588.
8. Crawford, *Scandinavian Scotland*, pp. 80–1.
9. A. A. M. Duncan, 'The dress of the Scots', *Scottish Historical Review*, 29 (1950), pp. 210–2.
10. D. E. R. Watt, *Biographical Dictionary of Scottish Graduates to AD 1410* (Oxford, 1977), pp. 374–5 for Malveisin and p. 485 for John the Scot, but on the latter, see also G. W. S. Barrow, 'The early charters of the family of Kinninmonth of that ilk', in *The Study of Medieval Records*, ed. D. A Bullough and R. L. Storey (Oxford, 1971), pp. 112–14; for Roger of Leicester, see *Regesta Regum Scottorum*, II, p. 30.
11. R. Somerville, *Scotia Pontificia*, nos 23–8, 31, 32.
12. D. E. R. Watt. 'Scottish university men of the thirteenth and fourteenth centuries', in *Scotland and Europe, 1200–1850*, ed. T. C. Smout (Edinburgh, 1986), pp. 10–11. For details of the individual cases, see Watt, *Biographical Dictionary*.
13. Watt, *Biographical Dictionary*, p. 168.
14. Dunbar, *Historic Architecture*, p. 147.

15. R Fawcett, *Jedburgh Abbey* (Historic Scotland, n.d.), pp. 14–15; Dunbar, *Historic Architecture*, p. 141.
16. Dunbar, *Historic Architecture*, pp. 20–3
17. For the de Vaux family, see Barrow, *Anglo-Norman Era*, pp. 20–2, 196; for these and other thirteenth-century castles, see Dunbar, *Historic Architecture*, pp. 23–33.
18. The best summary of medieval Scottish trade is in two essays in *The Scottish Medieval Town*, ed. M. Lynch, M. Spearman and G. Stell (Edinburgh, 1988): David Ditchburn, 'Trade with Northern Europe, 1297–1540', pp. 161–79; and Alexander Stevenson, 'Trade with the south, 1070–1513' pp. 180–206.
19. G. S. Pryde, *Burghs of Scotland.* To arrive at the figure of 55, the list of baronial burghs in Section II needs to be collated against the 38 royal burghs recorded in Section I before 1296, since many appear at differents dates in both lists.
20. Duncan, *Scotland*, pp. 514–15.
21. Barrow, *Kingship and Unity*, pp. 92–3.
22. Stevenson, 'Trade with the south', p. 187.
23. A. A. M. Duncan, 'The Scots invasion of Ireland, 1315', in *The British Isles, 1100–1500*, ed. R. R. Davies (Edinburgh, 1988), pp. 100–17.
24. Ditchburn, 'Trade with Northern Europe', p. 162.
25. Ibid., pp. 162, 163.
26. Watt, 'Scottish university men', p. 5.
27. For Mair's career, see J. Durkan and J. Kirk, *The University of Glasgow, 1451–1577* (Glasgow, 1977), ch. 9 and further references there cited.
28. Watt, 'Scottish university men', pp. 1, 5.
29. Francisque-Michel, *Les Ecossais en France, les Français en Ecosse* (2 vols, London, 1862); W. Forbes Leith, *The Scots Men-at-arms and Lifeguards in France, 1418–1830* (2 vols, Edinburgh, 1882).
30. *Fordun*, ed. Skene, p. 377, n. 3.
31. For these, and many other examples, see P. Contamine, 'Scottish soldiers in France in the second half of the fifteenth century: mercenaries, immigrants or Frenchmen in the making?', in *The Scottish Soldier Abroad, 1247–1967*, ed. Grant G. Simpson (Edinburgh, 1992), pp. 16–30; and the works cited above in note 29.
32. *Angels, Nobles and Unicorns; Art and Patronage in medieval Scotland* (National Museum of Antiquities of Scotland, Edinburgh, 1982), p. 32.

33. Ibid., p. 84; the other MSS mentioned are described ibid., pp. 84–7.
34. Ibid., pp. 88–90.
35. Reproduced in L. J. Macfarlane, *William Elphinstone and the Kingdom of Scotland* (Aberdeen, 1985), frontispiece.
36. *Angels, Nobles and Unicorns*, pp. 71, 74.
37. Ibid., pp. 37–8.
38. Ibid., pp. 36–7.
39. Ibid., p. 115.
40. Ibid., pp. 108–12.
41. Macfarlane, *William Elphinstone*, pp. 231–46.
42. Ian Campbell, 'A Romanesque revival and the early renaissance in Scotland, *c*. 1380–1513', *Journal of the Society of Architectural Historians*, 54 (1995), pp. 302–25. I am grateful to Dr Roger Mason for drawing my attention to this article.

EPILOGUE: A NEW AGE?

1. Macdougall, *James III*, pp. 152–80.
2. Jenny Wormald, *Court, Kirk and Community: Scotland, 1470–1625* (London, 1981), pp. 3–5.
3. Marcus Merriman, 'James Henrisoun and "Great Britain": British union and the Scottish commonweal', in *Scotland and England, 1286–1815*, ed. R. Mason (Edinburgh, 1987), pp. 85–112.
4. A. H. Williamson, *Scottish National Consciousness in the Age of James VI* (Edinburgh, 1979), especially chs 1 and 4.
5. Hector Boece, *Scotorum Historiae* (Paris, 1526).
6. Perhaps the real Richard Vairement, for whom see Watt, *Biographical Dictionary*, pp. 559–60.
7. George Buchanan, *De iure regni apud Scotos* (1579) and *Rerum Scoticarum Historia* (Edinburgh, 1582).
8. Williamson, *Scottish National Consciousness*, pp. 98, 108, 114–15.

SELECT BIBLIOGRAPHY

GENERAL

The best and most up-to-date one-volume history of Scotland is Michael Lynch, *Scotland: A New History* (London, first published 1991) which gives very full bibliographical references, as well as a most perceptive and thoughtful text. Briefer, but perhaps still the best introduction, is Rosalind Mitchison, *A History of Scotland* (London, 1970)

For a fuller treatment, turn to the series *The New History of Scotland*, first published by Edward Arnold in the 1980s. The first four volumes cover the period of this book: Alfred P. Smyth, *Warlords and Holy Men* (London, 1984); G. W. S. Barrow, *Kingship and Unity* (London, 1981); Alexander Grant, *Independence and Nationhood* (London, 1984); and Jenny Wormald, *Court, Kirk and Community* (London, 1981).

The volumes of the Edinburgh History of Scotland remain indispensable as the fullest modern treatment of Scottish history. For this period, see A. A. M. Duncan, *Scotland: The Making of the Kingdom* (Edinburgh, 1975) and Ranald Nicholson, *Scotland: The Later Middle Ages* (Edinburgh, 1974).

An essential biographical guide to many medieval Scottish churchmen is D. E. R. Watt, *A Biographical Dictionary of Scottish Graduates to AD 1410* (Oxford, 1977).

1 THE IDENTITY OF PLACE

For the archaeological background, see Graham and Anna Ritchie, *Scotland: Archaeology and Early History* (Edinburgh, 1991). A study of the distinctive features of Scottish architecture is J. G. Dunbar, *The Historic Architecture of Scotland* (London, 1966)

Two collections of essays on particular regions are *Galloway: Land and Lordship*, ed. R. D. Oram and G. P. Stell (1991) and *Moray: Province and People*, ed. W. D. H. Sellar (1993) (both published by the Scottish Society for Northern Studies, c/o The School of Scottish Studies, Edinburgh University).

On the early origin myths, which were to be so important in the later period, see E. J. Cowan, 'Myth and identity in early medieval Scotland', *Scottish Historical Review*, 63 (1984), pp. 111–35.

The best account of the Norse settlements is Barbara E. Crawford, *Scandinavian Scotland* (Leicester, 1987)

2 THE IDENTITY OF ORDER

For the development of Scotland in the twelfth and early thirteenth centuries, G. W. S. Barrow, *The Anglo-Norman Era in Scottish History* (Oxford, 1980) is fundamental; as are papers in the same author's *The Kingdom of the Scots* (London, 1973), especially those on 'The beginnings of military feudalism', 'Scotland's "Norman" families' and 'The earliest Stewarts and their lands'. On the relations of the crown with the western seaboard, see A. A. M. Duncan and A. L. Brown, 'Argyll and the Isles in the earlier middle ages', *Proceedings of the Society of Antiquaries of Scotland*, 90 (1956–7) pp. 192–220. On the thirteenth century, see D. E. R. Watt, 'The minority of Alexander III of Scotland', *Transactions of the Royal Historical Society* (5th series), 21 (1971) pp. 1–23; and important papers in *Scotland in Reign of Alexander III*, ed. Norman H. Reid (Edinburgh, 1990).

On the nobles, see *Essays on the Nobility of Medieval Scotland*, ed. K. J. Stringer (Edinburgh, 1985); and K. J. Stringer, *Earl David of Huntingdon: A Study in Anglo-Scottish History* (Edinburgh, 1985)

On urban history, see the essays in *The Medieval Scottish Town*, ed. M. Lynch, M. Spearman and G. Stell (Edinburgh, 1988); and the detailed study of one important town: E. P. D. Torrie, *Medieval Dundee* (Abertay Historical Society, Dundee, 1990)

The main documents on Anglo-Scottish relations are collected and translated in *Anglo-Scottish Relations, 1174–1328: Some Selected Documents*, ed. E. L. G. Stones (London and Edinburgh, 1965). See also the paper on 'The Anglo-Scottish border' in Barrow, *The Kingdom of the Scots.*

3 THE IDENTITY OF FAITH

The early period is best treated in Smyth, *Warlords and Holy Men*. The legend of St Andrew and its importance for Scotland is discussed in Ursula Hall, *St Andrew and Scotland* (St Andrews, 1994)

For the developments of the twelfth century, see the papers on the church in Barrow, *The Kingdom of the Scots*.

Papal bulls dealing with Scotland are listed, and where not otherwise available, printed, in R. Somerville, *Scotia Pontificia: Papal Letters to Scotland before the Pontificate of Innocent III* (Oxford, 1982). There is a short, but very useful introduction.

Ranging over the whole medieval period there is Ian B. Cowan, *The Medieval Church in Scotland*, ed. J. Kirk (Edinburgh, 1995). Many aspects of the fifteenth-century church are brought out in L. J. Macfarlane, *William Elphinstone and the Kingdom of Scotland, 1431–1514* (Aberdeen, 1985), an example of how much one can learn from a really good study of an individual, set in context.

4 THE WARS OF INDEPENDENCE

Essential is G. W. S. Barrow, *Robert Bruce and the Community of the Realm of Scotland* (use the 3rd edn, Edinburgh, 1988). The texts about the 'Great Cause' of 1291–2 are printed, with important introductory matter, in *Edward I and Throne of Scotland, 1290–1296* (2 vols), ed. E. L. G. Stones and Grant G. Simpson (Oxford, 1978). Other important documents are in *Anglo-Scottish Relations*, ed. E. L. G. Stones. On the Scottish mission to the papacy in 1301–2, see as well as Barrow, *Bruce* and *Anglo-Scottish Relations*, the article by R. G. Goldstein, 'The Scottish mission to Boniface VIII in 1301: a reconsideration of the context of the *Instructiones* and *Processus*', *Scottish Historical Review*, 70 (1991) pp. 1–15. On the Declaration of Arbroath, see the Historical Association pamphlet by A. A. M. Duncan, *The Nation of Scots and the Declaration of Arbroath* (London, 1970); and the article by Grant G. Simpson, 'The Declaration of Arbroath revitalised', *Scottish Historical Review*, 56 (1977) pp. 11–33.

For the reign of David II, as well as the Edinburgh History, there are two articles: Ranald Nicholson, 'David II, the historians and the chroniclers', *Scottish Historical Review*, 45 (1966) pp. 59–78, and Bruce Webster, 'David II and the government of fourteenth-century

Scotland', *Transactions of the Royal Historical Society* (5th series), 16 (1966) pp. 115–30.

5 THE NATIONAL IDENTITY

The best general guide is now the volumes of the series *The Stewart Kings of Scotland*, ed. Norman Macdougall. So far there have appeared: Michael Brown, *James I* (Edinburgh, 1994); Christine McGladdery, *James II* (Edinburgh, 1990); Norman Macdougall, *James III: A Political Study* (Edinburgh, 1982); and Norman Macdougall, *James IV* (Edinburgh, 1989). A volume on the early Stewart kings, Robert II and Robert III, by Stephen Boardman is imminently expected.

The most up-to-date discussions of the works of Fordun and Bower are in the introductions to the various volumes of the new edition of *The Scotichronicon of Walter Bower*, ed. D. E. R. Watt, which deal to some extent with Fordun as well as Bower. The projected volume IX will contain much fuller analyses and comments.

6 SCOTLAND AND CHRISTENDOM

Watt, *Biographical Dictionary* is essential for the links between some Scots and Europe. Some of his thoughts on Scottish graduates are distilled in the same author's 'Scottish university men of the thirteenth and fourteenth centuries', in *Scotland and Europe, 1200–1850*, ed. T. C. Smout (Edinburgh, 1986) pp. 1–18.

The subject of medieval Scottish trade is outlined in two papers in *The Scottish Medieval Town*: David Ditchburn, 'Trade with Northern Europe, 1297–1540', pp. 161–79, and Alexander Stevenson, 'Trade with the south, 1070–1513', pp. 180–206.

On the Scots in France in the fifteenth century, see P. Contamine, 'Scottish soldiers in France in the second half of the fifteenth century: mercenaries, immigrants or Frenchmen in the making?', in *The Scottish Soldier Abroad, 1247–1967*, ed. Grant G. Simpson (Edinburgh 1992) pp. 16–30.

On Scottish art and architecture in the middle ages, an excellent guide is the catalogue to a National Museum of Antiquities exhibition, *Angels, Nobles and Unicorns: Art and Patronage in Medieval Scotland* (Edinburgh, 1982).

Select Bibliography

SOURCES

Those who wish to tackle the sources of medieval Scottish history will have in the main to rely on the publications of the nineteenth-century historical clubs, and the official record publications, most of which are in the original language, usually Latin. Scottish royal charters to 1424 are being published in the series *Regesta Regum Scottorum*, of which four volumes have so far appeared, containing the 'acts' of Malcolm IV, William I, Robert I and David II. There is a discussion of all these sources and their problems in Bruce Webster, *Scotland from the Eleventh Century to 1603*, in the series 'The Sources of History' (London, 1975).

Some of the most important texts have, however, been translated. For the early period, the two works by A. O. Anderson, *Early Sources of Scottish History, AD500 to 1286* (2 vols, Edinburgh & London, 1922) and *Scottish Annals from English Chroniclers* (London, 1908) give comprehensive texts of the narrative sources in translation, split up into annals for particular years. *Anglo-Scottish Relations*, ed. Stones gives the main texts on its subject. There is a translation of the chronicle of John of Fordun in the series *The Historians of Scotland*, vol. 4 (Edinburgh, 1872) and of the Chronicle of Pluscarden, in the same series, vol. 10 (Edinburgh, 1880); while the new edition of the *Scotichronicon by Walter Bower*, ed. D. E. R. Watt and others (Aberdeen from 1987, and now Edinburgh from 1993) not only gives a translation of this large and wordy text, but notes which are an invaluable guide to other sources and literature.

There are very useful selections of the important texts, in translation, in *A Source Book of Scottish History*, ed. W. C. Dickinson, G. Donaldson and I. A. Milne (London & Edinburgh), I (1952) and II (1953).

CARTOGRAPHY

The maps at the start of this book are simply intended to clarify the text by locating places mentioned. There is a much more comprehensive cartographical account of medieval Scotland in *An Historical Atlas of Scotland c.400–c.1600*, ed. Peter McNeill and Ranald Nicholson (Atlas Committee of the Conference of Scottish Medievalists, 1975). This is unfortunately now out of print, but copies may be available in libraries, especially in Scotland. A new, much revised and enlarged, version has been in preparation for some years, and should be available before long.

The maps of Scotland in Blaeu's seventeenth-century Atlas (based on Timothy Pont's maps made in the late sixteenth century) have been very usefully reproduced in Jeffrey Stone, *Illustrated Maps of Scotland from Blaeu's Atlas Novus of the 17th Century* (London, 1991). They are important as the earliest comprehensive depiction of Scotland.

INDEX

157

Index

Index

Index

Index